Help Me Help My Child
A biblical counseling workbook for parents

Jenn Menn

Kimiko House
Cambridge

Subject Heading: PARENTING: RELIGIOUS ASPECTS: CHRISTIANITY
CHRISTIAN: BIBLE STUDIES

All scripture quotations, unless otherwise indicated, are taken from the Holy Bible, New International Version®, NIV®. Copyright ©1973, 1978, 1984, 2011 by Biblica, Inc.™ Used by permission of Zondervan. All rights reserved worldwide. www.zondervan.com The "NIV" and "New International Version" are trademarks registered in the United States Patent and Trademark Office by Biblica, Inc.™

This book is designed to provide accurate and authoritative information on the subject matter. It is sold with the understanding that the author is not engaged in rendering legal or professional services.

For the sake of simpler reading, all pronouns for child are formatted in masculine form.

Copyright © 2014 Jenn Menn All rights reserved.
Published by Kimiko House
100 Memorial Drive, St. 11-15A, Cambridge, Massachusetts 02142

Printed in the United States of America
FIRST EDITION

Cover image: DataCraft/Parents and Child/Getty Images

ISBN 978-0-9912478-1-3 (printed workbook)
ISBN 978-0-9912478-2-0 (ebook workbook)

Key words: CHILDREN, CHILD, KID, COUNSEL, COUNSELING, PARENT, PARENTING, HELP, CHRISTIAN COUNSELING

Help a Hurting Child.

Profits from this book help hurting children. This is done through foster care advocacy and by providing fundraising opportunities for families involving children with special needs, medical expenses, or financing adoption. Learn more or benefit from the work at www.jennmenn.com/fundraising. Help other hurt children by reviewing the book online, spreading the word, or help fundraise with the book for a family you know.

Contents

Note of Introduction 6

One: You First 11
Grace 12
Humility 15
Authority 17

Two: Taking a Look at Your Child 25
Personality 26
Health and Special needs 27
Learning Style 30
Skills 32
Emotions 35

Three: Your Child's Relationship with God 39
Word 42
Prayer 43
Worship 45
Faith, Hope, Love 47

Four: Your Child's Relationships with Others 49
Parenting Relationship 49
Trust and Obey Exercise 51
Other Relationships 61

Five: Your Child's Heart 65
Roots 65
Spiritual Warfare 72

Six: Your Child's Hurt 79
Weariness 81
Parent's role 83
Your Past Hurt 87
Humble Helper like Jesus 90
Promises 93
A Note on Jesus' Hurt 97
Addressing Hurt 98

Seven: Your Child's Sin 101
Pattern of sin 101
Cracking the code 108
Addressing specific sin 116
Discipline 119

Eight: Putting the Pieces Together 123
One at a time 123
Our great example 126
As a Child 127
Ways to Play 129
Back to the parent 132
Tips 134
Goal setting 135
Thanksgiving 137

Appendix 139
Searching Bible 140
Trust and Obey Chart 142
Roots Chart 143
My Child 147
Try it 148
Long term plans 151
Journaling 153
Coming in 2015 155
Bibliography 156

Note of Introduction

If you have picked up a book on biblical counseling for parents, I trust you want the best for your child. You want them to enjoy abundant life. In some seasons, that can become a muddled, mysterious path to navigate. Children, like adults, get out of whack. Sometimes we need outsiders to help address hurts or correct wrong thinking.

Maybe you have opened this workbook because your child has physical symptoms you think may be related to something going on in his heart or spirit. You have gone to the doctor and found no cause for the stomach aches, chest pains, rashes, sleeplessness, or bedwetting. Or possibly you opened this book because you have exhausted your bag of tricks but their disturbing behavior keeps occurring. You are trying to eliminate it, but the misbehavior springs up like a dandelion.

I also assume throughout the workbook, that you are a Christian. If you do not believe Jesus Christ died for your sins, has resurrected from the dead, and has given those who follow Him the Holy Spirit, this book may be confusing to you. Of course you are welcome to read on, but I would also encourage you to read the Bible to learn about God's love for you through Jesus Christ. Start in the section titled "John" rather than in the beginning at "Genesis." He gave His life so that you could have a relationship with God, which among many awesome things, will radically effect your parenting.

A lot of Christian parents want to be biblical parents. They strive to train their children in the way they should go, and seek to apply theological ideas and biblical truths to various aspects of their relationship with their child. This can be tricky because on the surface, Bible verses referencing 'child training' are hard to find, and may seem to give insufficient direction.

As a certified biblical counselor, I received numerous comments from parents over the years saying, "It's so hard to find a Christian counselor for children!" When I counsel children, I find it best to include the parents or caretakers, and then model interactions for parents to then do and say. The reason many counselors lean towards parental counseling is we recognize a parent's influence is more powerful than a counselor's influence.

Several aspects of the parent-child relationship make it powerful. For example parents have a special anointing of authority from God for their child. Also, the breadth and depth of interaction a parent has with his child far outweighs the counseling interactions. More so, parents are capable of counseling when given appropriate tools.

This workbook is a tool for parental counseling. It is not intended to be a thorough manual for comprehensive counseling: just a healthy boost. It will provide many questions you as a parent can use to discern what is wrong—sometimes without needing to ask your child and other times as prompts to ask your child. Children communicate loudly, and through intentional observation you may be able answer most questions. However, sometimes parents misinterpret the child or assume what he would say. Part of parents' responsibility is training their child to articulate what is going on in his head and heart. The questions in this workbook are for you the parent to answer, but use your discretion to re-word and ask your child if you think that will gain the best answer.

The questions and counsel through this book are not age specific. Most are applicable for toddlers through adolescents and many of those with special needs. Obviously, you know your child and I expect you to examine this material through the special, anointed lens you have as your child's parent.

This book is a tool to help you help your child. The result will be stronger character, a deeper relationship with your child, and a sense of restoration.

Take notes in the margins; several applications exist to allow you to write on the ebook digitally. Or, for either print or e-versions, consider recording answers in your journal so the workbook can be a template for future reference. The appendix contains worksheets to be copied or printed and written on as you work through the book as well.

Finally, Jesus calls the Holy Spirit a Wonderful Counselor. If you claim with your heart, mind, soul, and strength to believe in Jesus, you have received the Holy Spirit. Therefore as a Christian parent, you have a Wonderful Counselor inside of you to guide you in counseling your child. More so, we have the living, active, Word of God, which "is useful for teaching, rebuking, correcting and training in righteousness, so that the servant of God may be thoroughly equipped for every good work" (2 Timothy 3:16b-17).

May God use this workbook to equip you for the good work of counseling your child.

—Jenn

-ONE-
You First

Your capacity to counsel is directly related to your relationship with the Holy Spirit.

Jesus comforted His disciples with these words:

> "When he, the Spirit of truth, comes, he will guide you into all the truth."
> -John 16:13

Elsewhere, this Spirit of truth is referred to as Wonderful Counselor and Holy Spirit. Just before His death, Jesus reassured the disciples of divine guidance, knowing they would be confused in the days to come.

Likewise, parenting can be confusing and bring unexpected turns. Amidst them all, as a Christian, you have an incredible source of power and insight through the Holy Spirit. He is here to guide you—though sometimes that guidance will go against your natural inclinations and will require special submission. So take a deep breath and allow the peace of the Holy Spirit to encourage you. Your relationship with the Holy Spirit enables you to parent well.

Take a few minutes to consider the Holy Spirit's involvement in your current parenting efforts, and write your thoughts below.

With Grace

Grace implies provision of what we need and an attitude of contentment. In terms of provision, grace is the establishment of restored relationship with God, and all of the empowerment that follows. We are given so much of what we do not deserve: an intimate relationship with God including the Holy Spirit. If the provision of grace is an "input" from God, then an attitude of grace is our "output." Grace as an attitude is a key for training any child as well as preserving your own energy as a parent.

Because Christian parents want to raise moral children, we typically error towards presenting the part of religion that is the Law. But have we been able to live up to the Law? In parenting let us be reminded of this truth:

> "If you are led by the Spirit, you are not under the law...But the fruit of the Spirit is love, joy, peace, patience, kindness, goodness, faithfulness, gentleness, self-control; against such things there is no law. And those who belong to Christ Jesus have crucified the flesh with its passions and desires. If we live by the Spirit, let us also keep in step with the Spirit."
> -Galatians 5:18, 22-25

Everyone wants a child who is loving, joyful, peace patient, kind, good, faithful, gentle, and shows self-control. However, parents must not confuse these qualities themselves as the goal. Fruit it not the goal of a tree. Life is. Fruit is a byproduct of healthy living. Likewise, good 'fruit' in your child's life will be a byproduct of helping them keep in step with the Spirit. Qualities like gentleness and goodness cannot be hammered into your child any more than fruit can be hammered onto a tree. It may look pretty from a distance but it will not last.

I love the language ending the Galatians 5 verse: "keep in step." We all get a little off beat sometimes in our walk with the Lord, especially if we are not paying attention. Through paying attention to Him and His working by having regular time with the Lord, fellowship with others, and continual confession where we've fallen—we keep in step. As you go through this workbook, walk with the Lord: pray, read the Word, sing worship to Him.

The following pages will not fix your child any more than a self-help book will fix you. My goal here is to tune you into the Holy Spirit working in your child's life. To do so, you will need to be in step with the Spirit first, which is why these first sections focus on you.

Consider if your parenting is in step by reflecting on your last week of parenting. Have you been training your child more in understanding the Law or the Gospel?

For years, this verse was in front of my water filter. Every time I drank water, I was reminded:

> "God is able to make all grace abound to you, so that having all sufficiency in all things at all times, you may abound in every good work…He who supplies seed to the sower and bread for food will supply and multiply your seed for sowing and increase the harvest of your righteousness."
> -2 Corinthians 9:8,10 ESV

Through grace, we can do well and bear fruits of the Spirit in all things at all times. Grace energizes. If you are seeking help for your child, it is likely a trying time for you. Take heart that God knows and is providing for you. As you help your child, allow His grace to prevail in you.

Too often we either reject His grace or claim His grace as our own strength. Take a moment to pray, and ask God, "Show me a way You gave me grace this week?" Often your first thoughts are telling.

With Humility

Humility can be understood as the opposite of pride. When a person is humble, he is willing to seek forgiveness for shortcomings, consider others' interests over his own, and is open minded. Consider the following questions as a self-evaluation of pride in parenting.

When was the last time you sought forgiveness from someone for having offended them—whether you recognized it on your own or were corrected by others?

What about from your child?

Considering others' best interests is another telling piece of humility. Write about a recent time you considered others' best interests above your own desires:

Write about a recent time you considered your child's best interests above your own interests:

Being open-minded means not expecting or insisting upon our idea of what is right. Keep an open mind towards what the Holy Spirit is doing in your child with a spirit of open-minded humility. Annoying behavior is not necessarily sinful. What are a few considerations about your attitude to keep in mind as you go through this workbook?

Are there annoying (but not sinful) behaviors in your child you try to put down? If so, ask God for His special leadership in this area, so you may be joyful, loving, kind, and patient with your child.

God may be using your child's interests, personality, or voice to build your character as much as your child's. As the Lord brings to mind areas where you have fallen short in parenting, be quick to seek forgiveness from your child. Consider your child's interests above your own, and be open-minded to how the Spirit is at work.

With God given Authority

Parenthood has a rich presence throughout the Bible: God often addresses Himself as Father, He commands children to honor their parents in both the Old and New Testaments, and children are recognized as a heritage from the Lord. Understanding the role of God is central to understanding the role of parents.

A fundamental tenant of man's relationship with God is submitting to His authority. We have to know as Creator and King that He is in the place of authority to Judge. Man's identity hinges on God clarifying His role as the authority.

Satan was banished from heaven due to his rebellion from God's authority. Adam and Eve were separated of God's presence because of rebellion. At the heart of sin is rebellion: we think we know better than God. In contrast, Jesus says:

> "For I have come down from heaven not to do my will but to do the will of him who sent me."
> -John 6:38

Jesus understood authority.

Likewise, essential to your child's well-being is an understanding of authority: both towards parents, and ultimately towards our God. As a parent you are in a position to mold your child's understanding of the world, and authority in particular. Scholars of the Bible and followers of Christ consistently agree on the concept that parents have authority in order to point children towards an understanding of God's authority over man.

How has God revealed His authority to you?

In reading the following verses, what principles can you learn about how God demonstrates His authority in your own parenting?

John 14:21

1 John 5:3

Have you embraced the role of authority—parent—in your child's life?

What fears or cultural beliefs have kept you from embracing the role of authority in your child's life?

Are there ways in which you were parented that are keeping you from embracing authority?

More than any other person, a parent's role has a special authority in a child's life. Whether you are in place as a birth, foster, adoptive, or kinship parenting role, you are anointed by God as a parent to your child. You are in the divine position to help your child. As you work through these pages, I pray you step more confidently into your role of loving authority for the sake of your child, for the fulfillment of your parental responsibility, and for the peace of your home.

So as we begin to take a look at your child, may the grace of God be within you to the fullest, so you may consider and see your child as the Holy Spirit does. May He inform you and be your counselor in His perfect way.

With Character

A very popular verse for encouragement during difficult times is Romans 8:28. It says:

> "And we know that in all things God works for the good of those who love him, who have been called according to his purpose. For those God foreknew he also predestined to be conformed to the image of his Son"
> -Romans 8:28-29

Often people think of good to mean feeling happy, or having pleasant circumstances. In the verse, good is defined as becoming conformed to the image of Jesus. Character traits are the labels given to specify certain aspects of Jesus. So, growing in Christ-like character is good, and gives glory to God. Romans 8:28 is comforting because of a hope that God will use all circumstances for His purpose to conform us to Christ.

Ultimately, our pursuits are for the glory of God. Glory and worship are complex, as Paul discusses in Romans 5. One section of his discourse gives some perspective on your endeavor in helping your child.

> "Not only so, but we also glory in our sufferings, because we know that suffering produces perseverance; perseverance, character; and character, hope. "
> -Romans 5:3-4

The task of 'helping your child' infers a sort of suffering on both child and parent. Through the issues, troubles, and problems (as well as good times!), we have the opportunity to develop character, which will ultimately result in hope.

Below is a list of character qualities. Character is not innate: it is developed. Go through the list with your child in mind, and circle character traits you see being developed in him through the issues he is wrestling with.

Secondly, choose another color pen, or underline instead of circle, and mark the character you see developing in YOU as a result of the issue your child is wrestling with. You may wish to follow the pattern for each of your children and your spouse.

Appreciation	Attentiveness	Availability
Boldness	Commitment	Compassion
Confidence	Convictions	Cooperation
Courage	Creativity	Decisiveness
Deference	Dependability	Diligence
Discernment	Discipline	Encouragement
Endurance	Enthusiasm	Fairness
Faith	Flexibility	Generosity
Gentleness	Grace	Gratefulness
Honesty	Honor	Hope
Hospitality	Humility	Initiative

Joy	Kindness	Loyalty
Mercy	Observant	Orderliness
Patience	Peacemaker	Prudence
Reverence	Self-acceptance	Selflessness
Sensitive	Service	Sincerity
Tolerance	Thoroughness	Wisdom

God is working for the good of your child, and for your good too. And what is that good: happiness? worldly success? ease? No, it's character: conforming to the image of Jesus. Be encouraged, He's at work even now along this journey, not just at the endpoint. More so, His good work in your child is mutually beneficial for those your child interacts with.

Character produces hope (Romans 5:3-4). We live in a broken world so neither you nor your child will attain perfection until heaven. As you consider helping your child, know that he may not be able to be "fixed" but you can instill hope along the way.

With Truth (Prophesy)

> "Follow the way of love and eagerly desire gifts of the Spirit, especially prophecy… The one who prophesies speaks to people for their strengthening, encouraging and comfort… The one who prophesies edifies the church."
> -1 Corinthians 14:1,3,4

While the above passage is in the context of instructions for relationships within the church, your child is part of the church, and they will learn to relate with others from you.

Within the passage we find two commands. The first command is, "follow the way of love." The second command is, "eagerly desire gifts of the Spirit, especially prophecy."

Culture readily accepts the need for love in parenting. Prophecy is simply the telling of God's Word. The message can be revelation about the future, a warning of consequences for present actions, or relating truth to a past experience. It can be Scripture or a thought from the Holy Spirit.

Consider the passage above. The purpose of prophesy in the church is to strengthen, encourage and comfort. If you consider that your child is part of the church, then your child will be built up from your use of prophesy. While parenting will require many spiritual gifts, handling truth strengthens communication and facilitates a child's understanding of God. Prophecy and parenting go hand in hand. The daily upbringing of a child can only stay in line with God's will when each choice is saturated in the revealed, applied Word of God. This will strengthen, encourage, and comfort your child. If you want to be a strong Christian parent, prophecy is a means to do so.

Here are some ways to grow in the spiritual gift of prophecy:

A. Prophecy is a gift, so pray to God for it, for He gives good things to those who ask (Matthew 7:11).

B. If prophecy is sharing applicable Truth, then competency in knowing and applying the Word of God is essential. This comes by diligence and practice. Be in the Word often with attentive readings and studying. You will either be limited or equipped by the level of thoroughness with which you use the Word of God (2 Timothy 3:16).

C. Keep in step with the Spirit. Spiritual disciplines like worship, fellowship, prayer, reading of the Word, confession, and solitude help keep people in step with the Spirit.

-TWO-
Taking a Look at Your Child

Know your child

"Desire without Knowledge is no good: How much more will hasty feet miss the way"
-Proverbs 19:2

The technical counseling term for this first step is "data gathering." If you have ever been to a doctor, you know they have you fill out a medical history form and answer questions about what brings you there. The same is true with any diagnostic process.

In parenting, it may be tempting to breeze over this step, because you think you know your child. But bear with the process to gather some of this information into one place.

Let's begin with a prayer:

Holy Spirit bring to mind important aspects of my child as I answer the following questions. Remind me of the unique ways You have created my child and bring to mind any concerns You would like me to consider about my child. I commit this process to You and hope that even as I am seeking Your guidance to counsel my child, You Holy Spirit are tending to his heart. Thank you for being a Wonderful Counselor.

First, is there a specific problem that brings you to this book?

What do you hope your child gains by you reading this book? Write your answer below, and then record a simple phrase to represent this in the "My Child" chart (found in the appendix to copy or tear out).

Your Child's Personality

Hopefully thinking about your child's personality brings a smile to your face. God uniquely created every child with certain traits for certain purposes. Even though parents may prefer or reject certain traits, each personality trait is useful and none is better or more useful than another in itself. Circle the qualities below which best describe your child:

Active	Sober-minded	Ambitious
Self-confident	Persistent	Relaxed

Crafty	Hardworking	Loyal
Impulsive	Independent	Excitable
Imaginative	Dependent	Calm
Serious	Easy-going	Strong-willed
Shy	Good-natured	Introvert
Extrovert	Timid	Leader
Quiet	Tough	Spiritual
Self-conscious	Lonely	Attentive
Rough	Sensitive	Moody
Fun	Nice	Helpful

Any others:

Choose the two most prevalent personality traits of your child that you circled and record them on the "My Child" chart.

Health and Special Needs

Does your child have a chronic illness/disease?

Does your child take any medication?

List the side effects your child seems to experience from this medication. (ask him/her if needed).

Has your child been diagnosed with any mental health issues? If so, is the diagnosis considered a lifetime issue?

Besides those already mentioned, does your child have special-needs to consider throughout this book (handicaps, genetic disorders, injuries, prior abuse, puberty)?

How does your child seem to feel or react to these illnesses/ side effects/ mental health/ special needs he experiences?

What extra challenges might your child face because of any health or special need considerations? (Choose from the list on the following page and write any unique considerations for your child.)

Less free time because of treatment

Chores or school work is challenging

Unable to participate in activities (List how so in margin)

Insecurity

Lower level of functioning (List how so in margin)

Any others:

Summarize your answers from the Health and Special Needs section in the "My Child" chart.

Your Child's Learning Style

In the columns below place checkmarks next to the attributes describing your child. Note, the heading of the column that has the most items checked. This title represents his preferred learning style. Record this style on the "My Child" chart, along with the top few phrases of how he learns from the list.

Auditory	Visual	Kinesthenic
Picks up music lyrics	Likes books	Often moving
Listens to conversations	Likes TV	Makes messes
Completes sentences	Notices billboards	Multi-tasks
Retells stories heard	Draws/paints	Experiments
Asks lots of questions	Tells of images seen	Volunteers to try
Plays instruments	Journals/doodles	Crafty
Uses dramatic voice	Unscrambles puzzles	Spontaneous
Debates	Likes collages	Body language
Responds to verbal commands	Prefers lists	Mimics

What are your child's favorite toys?

What are you child's favorite activities/ways to play (i.e. imaginative, role-playing, interactive games, sports, crafts)?

Record a few of these toys and activities under "playing favorites" on the My Child worksheet.

Rank the style which best represents the way your child best takes in and responds to love. 1 being most important and 4 being least important.

____Words (conversation, affirmation)

____Physical Affection (smiles, hug, massage, kiss, hand holding, eye contact)

____Activities (recreation, time together, serving)

____Objects (gifts, sharing, playing with an object)

Record the #1 style on the My Child Worksheet

When your child is offered seemingly pleasant activities, experiences, or relationships, does he usually engage in them?

When your child is offered nurturing touch whether through direct affection, in games, or treatment when hurt, does he seem comfortable, or resist it?

In considering these matters, do you have any additional comments or insights to note about the way your child learns?

Your Child's Skills

Considering an open range of age-appropriate skills or tasks, what are your child's strengths in:

- academics: reading, writing, math, science?

- fine-motor: piecing together, hand-eye coordination?

- gross-motor: movements, sports, coordination?

- skills needed for his hobbies?

What skill weaknesses do you perceive in your child?

What are a few challenging tasks or skills your child faces right now (i.e. writing his name, catching a football, putting clothes away)? Is the challenge that he is not able to perform the task or one that he is not willing to face?

How does your child respond to these challenges?

What structures are in your child's life for play and education (places like school, day care; teams or clubs, playground, video game system, playroom, set times for activity-x, etc.)?

How does your child respond to these structures?

In considering your child's skills, do you have any additional comments or insights to note?

Record a summary of challenges and strong skills on the My Child worksheet.

Your Child's Emotions

Children are immature. They have not yet learned how to identify or express emotions properly, either in word or action. Part of childhood is developing and practicing self-expression. Sometimes a child's behavior is an expression of what he is feeling. Actions and attitudes that seem to be out of line with your child's general personality usually mean your child is using the behavior for expression (whether intentionally or not). They are like symptoms. Go through the list of attitudes and actions to mark any of the following behaviors that currently characterize your child. Jot down an example of each behavior you select next to the term (i.e. Sensitive- cries when we leave home).

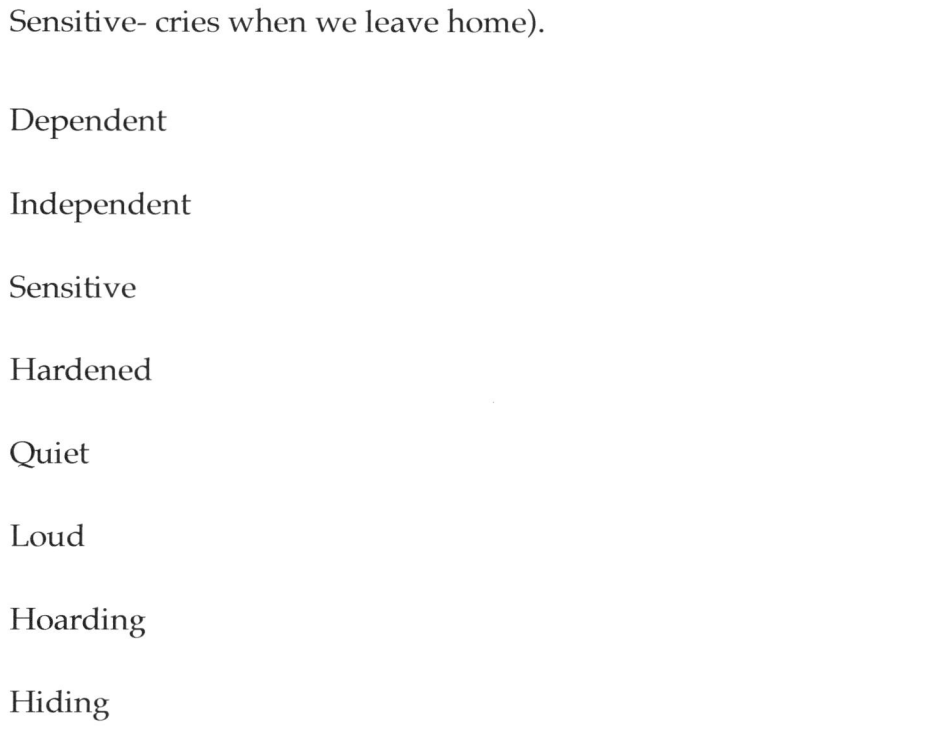

Dependent

Independent

Sensitive

Hardened

Quiet

Loud

Hoarding

Hiding

Taking from others

Passive

Demanding

Apathetic

Destructive

Reckless

Place a star next to behaviors above that trouble you.

What emotion(s) might your child be trying to express in the behaviors you selected?

Angry/Mad	Confusion	Excitement
Joy	Frustration	Fear/Scared
Jealousy	Worry	Uncertainty
Peaceful/Relaxed	Powerful/Confident	Resentment
Bitterness	Insecure	Sad/depressed

Can you pinpoint when the troublesome behavior or emotions began to appear?

Is this behavior an age appropriate expression? (Whether or not the behavior is age appropriate helps you empathize and bear through the growth process with patience. However, being age appropriate does not excuse the behavior if it is sinful.)

Has your child had any changes in his life recently? Think about circumstances or relationships that may seem insignificant and might otherwise be overlooked by you. These can be both positive and negative changes. For example, one of my children came home from school every day for a week exhausted and teary. It turns out she had a substitute teacher, and that change affected her. Changes in friends, church, siblings, a room change, or new responsibilities like chores all should be considered. Other, bigger changes might be moves, new school, death of a family member, parental separation, parental military deployment, and the like. List changes that your child is experiencing here:

What changes have you, the parent, had in your life recently (new relationships, job responsibilities, chores, health)? A significant cause of failure for me in parenting was when I did not realize a stressor in my life added to my child's stress.

Every change, even positive changes has a loss. For example, graduating into high school is an accomplishment but comes with the loss of familiarity and maybe loss of some close friends or teachers. Losses can be relational, the removal of possibility, changes in surroundings, or changes in circumstances. What losses may your child be experiencing as a result of the changes you listed above?

Think about a time in your child's life when they experienced a major change in the past: how did he react (emotion, attitude, or actions) then?

Do you see any similarities in current ways he is expressing himself?

In considering your child's emotions and changes, do you have any additional comments or insights to note?

-THREE-
Your Child's Relationship With God

Every individual is meant for an intimate relationship with Jesus Christ.

This begins with an understanding of God's grace to replace guilt with innocence, shame with honor, and fear with power. Helping your child through any circumstance or attitude will be in vain unless it is built on the foundation of God.

Describe your child's relationship with God.

What does your child understand about the authority of God?

What does your child understand about the work of Jesus Christ?

What does your child know about the Holy Spirit?

How does your child seem to connect with God?

The following questions may contain "deep" concepts that even some adults struggle to grasp, but children can begin to gain basic understanding of these principles between ages 5 and 8.

Would you say your child believes in the salvation of his sins through faith in Jesus Christ?

Would you say your child has hope of his place of honor as an heir of God, cleansed from shame (who he is in Christ)?

Does your child recognize the power of trusting in Jesus over all things?

These questions expose key elements of living in relationship with God. A whole, healthy spiritual life is difficult to maintain without them. For example, if your child understands guilt but not salvation, despair and anxiety may be present in him. Likewise, if your child lacks an understanding of who he is in Christ, you can expect your child to be living in some level of shame. Finally, if your child sees evil and suffering but does not know Jesus' power, fear will likely surface.

These are areas to start with in helping your child—helping him know about Jesus Christ in these ways. These are central themes in the Bible. Jesus Christ brings justification, honor, and power. I am scratching the surface of these complex concepts so you can see your child, like all Christians, have more to learn than the "Jesus loves me" song. Though he may not be of age to conceptualize the fullness of the matters, start (or keep) teaching him. Play, advice, assurances, training, and the like will help your child, but lasting measures will come when he has a strong foundational understanding of the Gospel.

People grow in their understanding and relationship with God through a number of ways. The next few pages are dedicated to considering how you as a parent can help your child cultivate faith.

The Word of God

"Faith comes from hearing the message, and the message is heard through the word of Christ."
-Romans 10:17

The Bible is the main form of the Word of God. The Bible contains the explanation of the gospel of Jesus Christ, which has the power of God to drastically change our lives. Besides instructions for moral living, the Bible can be the Holy Spirit's way to speak into our lives to bring whatever we need: healing, correction, training, or wisdom.

How are you, as a parent, receiving the Word in your life?

How is your child currently receiving the Word is his life?

How can you facilitate your child better receiving the Word in his life this week? (Circle as many as appropriate)

Board/card games   Conversation

Family devotion time   Providing time alone for him to

Three: Your Child's Relationships with God

	read and think about the Bible
Bible-verse songs	Christian radio
Listening to sermons	Christian literature
Church/club attendance	Other:

What Scriptural Truth could you share with your child this week? For help on searching for topics in the Bible see the appendix page "Search the Bible." We will dive into this more in future sections as well.

For any choice you circled above or Scripture you thought of, record it on the "Try it!" Worksheet found in the Appendix. By the end of the book, this worksheet will provide a summary of various ideas to help your child.

Prayer

Prayer is communication with God for the sake of intimacy, understanding, adoration, giving thanks, peace, and asking for help. It can be done in a variety of ways: silently or out loud, alone or with others, on your knees or as you drive, orally or written, brief or at length, in song or narrative.

Describe your own prayer life.

Describe your child's prayer life.

What is your child thanking God for?

What is your child asking God?

How can you help your child develop a deeper prayer life? Circle those you can commit to help him with this week.

Model praying. When?

Ask him to pray. When?

Create a prayer journal guide for him.

Three: Your Child's Relationships with God

Schedule journaling prayer time.

Create a "thankful jar" or chain to note prayers of thanksgiving.

Create an "asking jar" to note questions, prayer requests or anxieties.

Share stories of prayer and answered prayer (both in the Bible, biographies, and current).

Other:

For any choice you circled, record it on the "Try it!" Worksheet.

Worship

> "The hour is coming, and now is, when true worshippers will worship the Father in spirit and in truth, for the Father is seeking such to worship Him. God is a spirit and they that worship Him must worship Him in spirit and in truth."
> -Jesus in John 4:23-24

Meditating in the Bible and praying are examples of worship, but many other things people say or do are worship as well. Any activity where the intention of the heart is to express recognition, love or gratefulness to God is worship.

Parent: How are you worshipping God in your life?

How does your child worship God?

How can you provide space/opportunity for your child to worship God?   (Circle)

Encourage current activities   Church participation

Family devotion time   Singing

Artistic performances   Thankfulness craft/journals

Make down time   Play worship music

Other:

For any choice you circled, record it on the "Try it!" Worksheet.

Faith, Hope, and Love

"For now we see only a reflection as in a mirror; then we shall see face to face. Now I know in part; then I shall know fully, even as I am fully known. And now these three remain: faith, hope, and love. But the greatest of these is love."
-1 Corinthians 13:12-13

Scripture tells us that right now we see, know, and have gifts and skills only "in part," like a reflection of complete life. Certain skills will last eternally, when all other knowledge, skills, and gifts pass: these are faith, hope and love. If faith, hope and love will last, then surely they are helpful and valuable to complete living.

Therefore, let us consider how you can help develop faith, hope, and love in your child. Faith is an assurance in the LORD: who He is and trust in how He works. Growing in knowledge and relationship with God as we discussed develops faith.

Hope is a desire and anticipation for the fulfillment of something. Hope is encouraging and motivating. Read Romans 15:4-13. What are some ways that the passage tells us we can develop hope?

You child needs hope. Hope is a producer of joy and peace (Verse 13). When your child has a hurt, sin, or is under spiritual attack, he is like a bucket with a hole in it. Peace and joy drain out of the hole so he will need continual replenishment—more than normal. So remember to provide encouragement through acceptance of your child as he grows. Hope is key.

Besides faith and hope is love. This is developed in relationship with God, and in relationship with others. Since we considered your child's relationship with God in this chapter, in the next section we will consider your child's relationship with others.

-FOUR-
Your Child's Relationships With Others

A child is affected and developed through relationships with others.

The relationships a child maintains are critical to his development. Childhood interactions have long-lasting effects. In this section you will describe elements of parental relationships as well as survey other relationships in your child's life that impact him.

Parents

How would you describe the father's relationship to your child?

How would you describe the mother's relationship to your child?

How would your child describe his relationship with father?

How would your child describe his relationship with mother?

Your child may also have step-parent or birth-parent relationships. Describe those below. (Later in the section you will have an opportunity to describe other important relationships your child has as well.)

While the Bible has much to say about how to interact in relationships, a summary would be to love others. First Corinthians 13 says the following qualities describe love:

Patient	Kind	Not jealous
Not boastful	Not proud	Not dishonoring
Not self-seeking	Not easily angered	No record of wrongs

Not delight in evil	Rejoices with Truth	Protects
Trusts	Hopes	Perseveres

Go back to the parental relationships described above and beneath each jot the elements of love you see as part of each relationship. Now use a red pen and list aspects of a loving relationship that your child is missing under each relationship. The person at fault is irrelevant at this point: for example, whether the step-father or child is responsible for being easily angered, write "not easily angered."

Next is an exercise to look deeper and provide insight for improving these relationships.

Trust and Obey Exercise

In the Bible, we often read of the partnership of faith and deeds. When we have faith, good works flow from the Holy Spirit. Faith and deeds are two sides of the same coin. Another way to phrase this is "Trust and Obey." Faith and trust require a belief in promises or assurances, where deeds and obedience are a by-product of faith and trust.

Read 2 Peter 1:3-11 and pay attention to the mix of promises and commands. In verses 3-4, we learn that God has given us everything we need to obey, and He backs up his asks of us with promises. So, He has given us reason to trust.

Then, in verses 5-9 we "add to your faith goodness, and to goodness knowledge…" The Greek word for faith is 'pistis,' meaning more direct reliance upon Christ. So, we are to add to our reliance upon Christ these other things, not for our salvation, but rather for successful growth. He says: "If you do these things, you will never fall." (Verse 10)

Wow: NEVER fall. Wouldn't that be great? You may be going through this workbook because your child is "falling" into inappropriate behaviors. Or maybe you as a parent continue to fall. Faith and goodness keep your family on a track of knowledge, self-control, perseverance, godliness, kindness, and love that will result in effective and productive parenting.

Write the section of 2 Peter 1:3-11 which is most encouraging or hopeful for you here:

The beginning of an effective, productive life is to grow in faith and goodness. Trust and obey by the power of God.

A person's relationship with God is not to be relegated to personal reading time or church. A relationship with God should permeate every area of life, including relationships. Trusting and obeying, therefore, should be applied to relationships too.

On the next few pages is a tool to help sort through some complicated areas of a relationship. Every relationship has two-sides: certain aspects that we can control and are responsible for, and other aspects that may concern you but are out of your control. For those you can control, we are calling them areas to obey. For those you cannot control, we are calling them areas to trust.

Within the square below, you write phrases in either the inner or outer shape. The inner square is the area that the individual is responsible for. These are areas to obey. The outer square represents all aspects of the relationship that are of concern to you, but are not your responsibility. The shapes together represent one side of an individual relationship. For example a mom would place in the inner square phrases describing how she is to act, think, or react in her relationship with her child. The concerns listed in the outer circle are areas for the mom to surrender and trust God in regards to her child. She cannot control them.

The exercise will bring awareness of what you actually believe you are responsible for. When you properly live out your responsibilities, and leave what was never meant for you to carry as a concern for prayer, some tension will naturally be lifted. It may free both you and your child in areas you did not realize were burdensome. Sometimes awareness will correct areas of your relationship. Other times, these shapes will serve as references to hold you accountable and guide your prayers.

First complete the inner shape: what are some things you feel or know you are responsible for as your child's parent? If something comes to mind as important, but does not fit under your responsibility, jot it in the outer square. The more specific you brainstorm, the better. Next, bring to mind any concerns or other areas of your child's life you CARE about but are not RESPONSIBLE for. The first figure below is an example, and you may record many of the same phrases on yours. A separate chart should be completed by each parent.

Four: Your Child's Relationships

Trust

Salvation

His relationship with his step-dad

Safety at school, with friends

Obey

Love/Respect Spouse
Help with homework
Read Bible & pray with
Love: patient, kind, forgiving, protect
Support his achievements
Discipline him
Teach him right and wrong
Be involved in his friendships
Keep him safe
Provide for his needs: food, housing, affection
Help ensure he's health

how he treats others/ integrity

he tells the truth

how well he does at school

happiness

success

his anxiety

his thoughts stay pure

Dad to Child

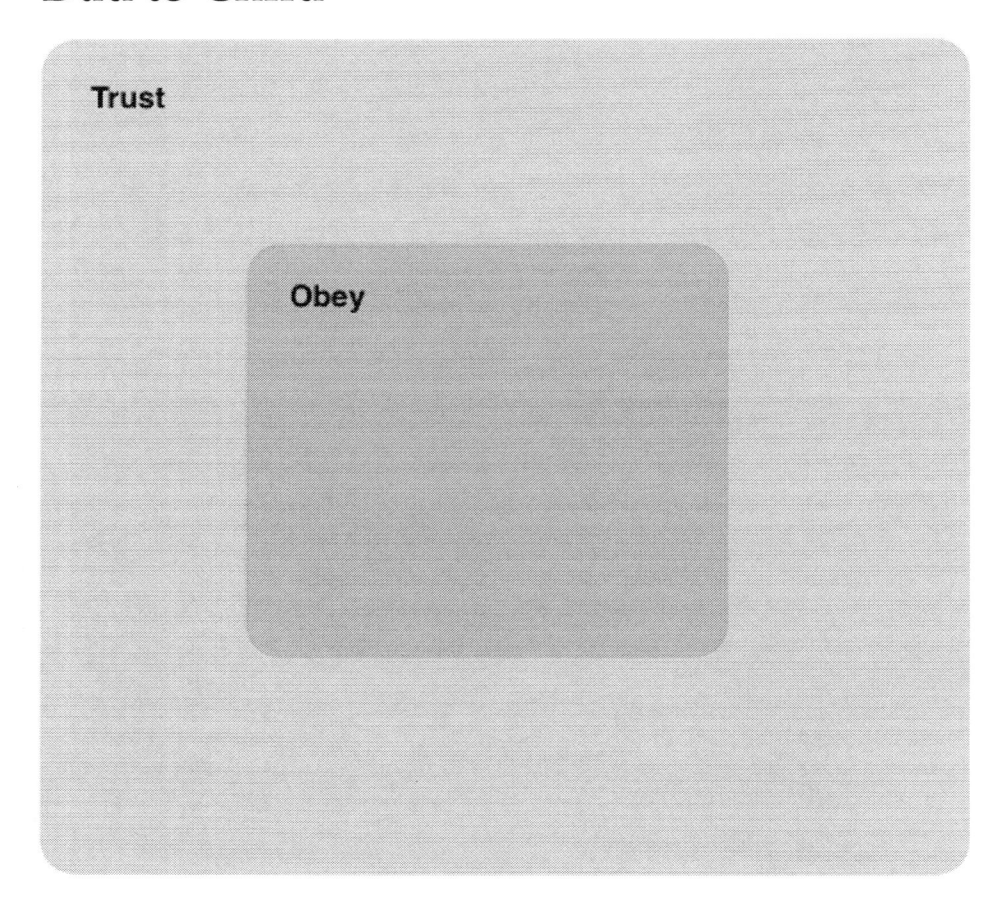

Trust

Obey

Mom to Child

Trust

Obey

Next Steps:

1. Go back to the inner, obey square, and underline responsibilities you wrote that are found in the Bible. Place a Scripture reference next to it (refer to the appendix on how to search the Bible).

Any terms that are not drawn from Scripture are cultural. For example, reading stories to your child is cultural. It may be a good effort, but it is not a biblical responsibility. The parent-child relationship can strain when parents pressure children in areas that are not biblical. Either the parent or child feels exacerbated. This means the problem gets worse. Reflect on your 'obey' square. Have you been burdening yourself or your child by placing many responsibilities on parenting that are not biblical? If so, how may this be effecting your child? How may this be effecting you?

2. In reflection, if you think any of the things you wrote in the 'obey' square belong in the outer shape, draw an arrow connecting the word to the 'trust' shape. These may be either biblical or cultural aspects of your relationship

3. Now look to the outer trust area. Remember, these are things that may be important, but you are not supposed to be in control of. They are things to rely on God about. "Cast all your cares upon God, because He cares for you" (2 Peter 5:7). Spend a minute praying to God acknowledging your commitment to trust Him in these areas of your child's life.

4. You have looked at one side of the relationship. Now, identify your child's areas to trust and obey in the shape below. Use a red pen for the responsibilities and concerns from your child's perspective, and blue for the parent's perception of what his list should be. Ask your child, "What are things you are in control of, or responsible for, between me and you, or you and mom? Then, what are some other things about us that matter to you, but aren't really up to you to control?" If your child is young, you may wish to draw pictures for phrases as you discuss responsibilities and concerns so that he can better understand.

    The differences may be surprising. Use this exercise as a way to communicate with your child about expectations you differ on. Consider the differences in relationship expectations your child has of himself. How might they be influencing your relationship with one another?

Child to Parents

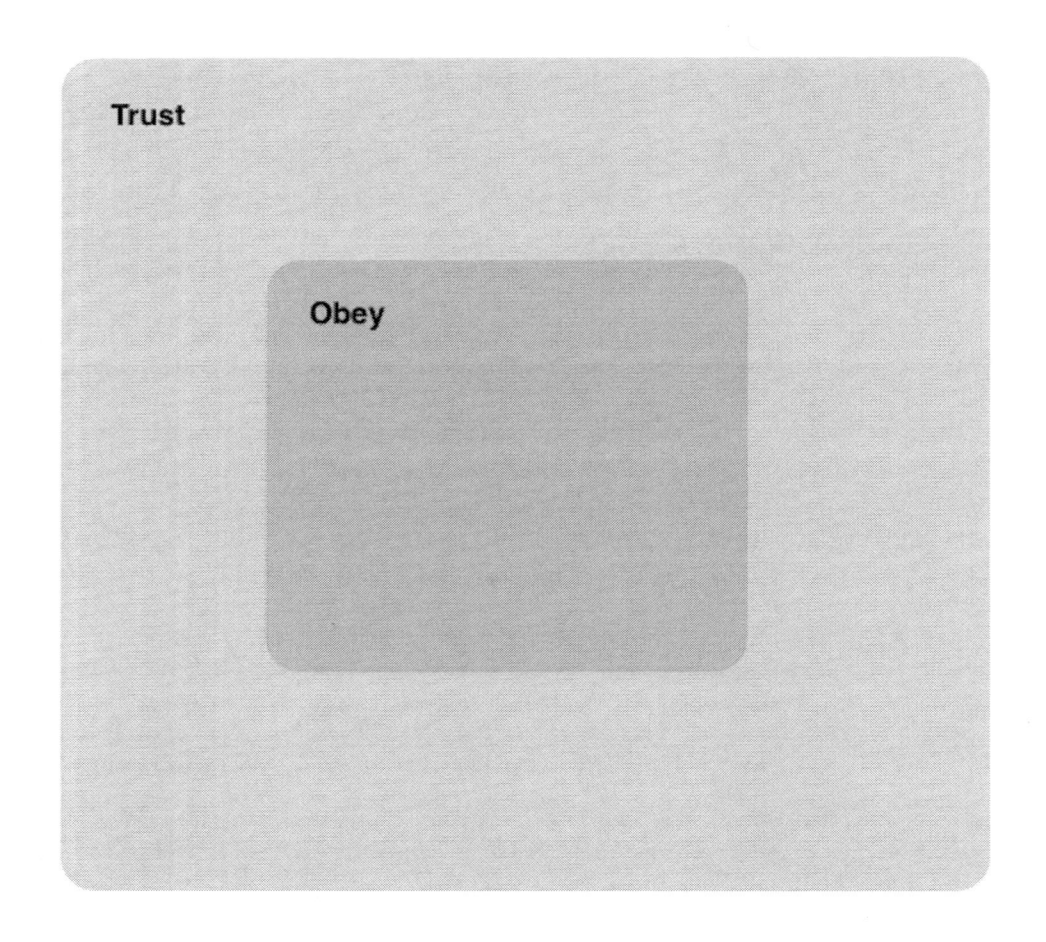

Trust

Obey

Others

You and your child likely have other relationships that deeply matter to your child and influence how your child is thinking, feeling, and acting.

1. List the names and relationship of other key people in your child's life, leaving room in between to come back and make comments.

i. Older individuals: (step-parents, grandparents, relatives, teachers, mentors, siblings)

ii. Peers/younger individuals: (sibling close in age, neighbors, playmates, who your child sits next to in school)

2. Certain relationships are stronger than others.
i. Circle, or add to the list the names of those your child lives with.
ii. Underline the top five people overall you think are most important to your child.
iii. Ask your child who are the most important people in his life right now and note those with a star.

3. Go through the list and comment on any observations you have about how that relationship is going. Have you observed a special closeness, or problems? How loving are the relationships, with 1 Corinthians 13 in mind?

4. Place one word near each name you would use to characterize their relationship.

Note: Some of these relationships, such as siblings, may have such complexity that your time would be well spent to grab a piece of paper and do the charting "Trust and Obey" exercise for your child in that relationship. You also may want to ask your child open-ended questions about their relationships with specific people, like, "How are things going with Shelly?" or "How are you and your sister getting along these days?" An extra blank shape is in the Appendix.

-FIVE-
Your Child's Heart

Roots

When you see an apple, regardless of whether you picked it from the farm or bought it from the store, you know it came from the branch of a tree. That branch is attached to the trunk, which is supported by roots. The tree uses roots to draw nourishment from the ground and water. The leaves use the sun's energy to also help the branch produce fruit.

Likewise, fruit in our lives originates from nourished roots and healthy leaves, even when the fruit seems to be disconnected. Without strong roots, we have a hard time bearing fruit. The Bible speaks to this concept in several places. Take, for example, Jeremiah 17:7-8:

> "Blessed is the man who trusts in the Lord whose trust is the Lord. He is like a tree planted by water, that sends out its roots by the stream, and does not fear when heat comes,
>   for its leaves remain green, and is not anxious in the year of drought, for it does not cease to bear fruit."

The Scripture provides the imagery of a healthy tree to show that a man who trusts in the Lord can stand firm amidst troublesome circumstances because he draws his strength and nourishment from below the surface.

Reflect on the data you have gathered on your child and relate it to this imagery: Does your child know there is water to draw from? Are your child's perception, relationships, hurts, circumstances or sins like heat causing fear or withering? Is your child a developing tree that just needs support to grow over time? What fruit can you see of his trust in the Lord? Whatever the trouble is, your child has the potential to be an oak of righteousness for the Lord, rooted and established in His love, and bearing the fruit of life for others (Isaiah 61:3).

Disappointments

Disappointment is the feeling that follows a failure of expectations or hopes to come true. Disappointment may appear as bitterness, shyness, hyperactivity, tears, anger, selfishness, and other behaviors or attitudes. These symptoms of disappointment indicate something is troubling your child's heart. With this in mind, reflect on the insight you gained from Taking a Look at your Child. Does your child seem to have any disappointments about:

His personality?

His health or special needs?

His learning?

His skills?

His emotions?

What disappointments does your child seem to have in relationships with (fill in other key relationships from previous section):

God:

Dad:

Mom:

(   ):

(   ):

(   ):

Look back through the list of what you have written in this section on disappointments. Circle any which seem to be related to the same issue. How would you label that disappointment? Record the label on the Roots Chart in the appendix.

Consider those left without a circle: Can you see a different correlation between those disappointments? Underline those, and record a label on the chart too, each 'grouping' under a new column

Refer back through the list of emotions your child is expressing. Can you see any correlation between the emotion and disappointment? Re-write any emotion next to the disappointment it relates to on the Chart.

Expectations

Usually, people are disappointed because they expected a certain outcome—whether that be an action, response, or attitude that went unmet. For example, Millie was disappointed because she thought having a baby sister would be fun but it turns out that she cries a lot, cannot play, and steals Mom's attention all the time.

Answer the questions in this section for each labeled disappointment on the chart, and fill in the answers on the Chart. Start with the first disappointment and answer all questions in the Expectations section. Then, return here and begin the questions for the next disappointment: What could your child have been expecting that's led to their disappointment?

Expectations come from our beliefs. We think, or perceive, through our life's lens something we want, need, or should avoid. In the example above, Millie developed an expectation of what having a baby sister would be. She heard 'baby sister' and thought of her dolls she played with all the time. Her dolls did not take away mom's attention or cry. How do you think your child came to his/her expectations listed above? Do you think your child perceives this expectation as a need?

We are looking at disappointments and expectations because they are often indicators of:
- Lies your child is believing
- Areas where he is taking worship away from God and giving it to something else (idolatry)
- Hurts he may have
- How to handle the sin he is caught up in

As you think about your child's disappointments and expectations, can you articulate any underlying lies he may be believing that would lead toward his disappointment or expectation?

Without the self-control from the Holy Spirit, we all tend to convert good things into wants, then into needs, and then into our "MUST haves." Once an area reaches the mind-set of "must have," it is what the Bible calls an "idol." An idol is anything or anyone we deem so important it becomes our priority to satisfy it above all else. This act is essentially worship: worship refers to our place of joy, what we sacrifice for, where we place time and energies. For example, your child's baseball abilities, or his Xbox may be idols he worships. What things or people has your child made a "MUST have" (or an idol)?

Go back through this Expectations section again if you have multiple disappointments on the Roots Chart, considering each issue/disappointment in turn.

Two big things may be going on in your child's heart if he is troubled: hurt and sin. So, you are about to focus in extensively to figure out how you can help your child in his hurt and/or with regards to his sin.

    Addressing the hurt comes first. This is the way Jesus often treats us. Read the Gospel of John with eyes to see this pattern. As you read how Jesus interacts with people, ask yourself: 'How is He addressing their hurt, and how is He addressing their sin?'

Spiritual Warfare

One important consideration amidst all this is the battle between good and evil. We see it in the movies, in news, and in Scripture. It is in our lives too. Spiritual warfare is the common Christian term for the involvement of evil forces in the world. Evil causes hurt and often gains strength to attack through temptation and sin. While this workbook is not going to discuss in depth this rather mystical aspect of life, I would be failing to provide thorough help if I neglected to mention it.

Victory over evil can happen through one's attitude. For example, Satan provoked Job using circumstances, but his attitude proved faithful. Despite destruction, financial loss, disease, death—Job defeated evil using his continuing faith in God and refusal to harden himself towards the Lord. The attack was at the physical level but the victory was determined in Job's heart. This same pattern occurs with many characters of the Bible: ruin in the physical but victorious by the spirit (Job, Hannah, Jesus, Paul, apostles, Hagar, to name a few).

So, the world is not the battleground: we are the battleground. Pride, vanity, anger, terror, satisfaction, power, envy, quarreling, deception, sexual perversion, and bitterness can each be attitudes provoked by evil. Evil seeks to cause you and your children to have bad attitudes toward the Lord and His good things.

Paul speaks plainly about these matters in Ephesians 6:10-18.

There we read how we are to stand firm against evil. In addition to prayer, Paul lists several pieces of armor we should put on to guard ourselves. I do not know of any evidence suggesting this armor was physical. Rather, the pieces of armor are symbolic of attitudes and beliefs that protect us. The following questions help you consider how you can protect your family against evil using the "Armor of God." Answer each in the context of your child's situation or circumstances.

A. Truth

Truth refers to God's standard of what is true and what is false. How can you defend yourself and child with truth?

Would you say your child is protected by an understanding of truth about his situation/circumstances?

B. Righteousness

Righteousness is a state of being sinless: being right in all our thinking and doing. Ultimately, righteousness only comes from Jesus Christ, and then the work of sanctification begins—His calling for righteous living. Is there any known wrongdoing in your life or your child's life that would leave you and him unprotected?

C. Peace

Peace comes in understanding of the message of Christ's power over evil and His sovereignty in all things. The divine presence of God, through disciplines like prayer, brings peace. How can you protect yourself and child with Peace?

Would you say your child has a sense of spiritual peace about his situation?

D. Faith

"Now faith is confidence in what we hope for and assurance about what we do not see" (Hebrews 11:1). It comes from a belief God is who He says He is, and will do what He promises. Would you say your child knows and believes God and His promises (faith)?

How can you arm yourself and child with faith?

E. Salvation

Salvation from sin and the grip of evil came through Jesus Christ. Have you and your child called on the name of Jesus Christ for salvation?

F. Word of God

The Word of God (Bible) is called the Sword of the Spirit. The Bible can be used to combat evil: when you believe and speak the words of God, it cuts the power evil has in your life. Would you say your child knows how to use the Bible against evil?

G. Prayer

Prayer is not referenced as a piece of armor, but it is emphasized as being critical to standing firm against evil. Would you say you use prayer to stand firm?

Would you say your child uses prayer to stand against evil?

All considered, how well are you and your child protected with the Armor of God?

Look at the Roots Chart and consider: how could these issues be protected against in the future with the elements of the Armor of God. Write any ideas in the "Armor of God" row.

No question about it, evil will attack your child. You may or may not recognize it when it happens, but being intentional in wearing the Armor of God will help you and your child stand firm when it happens.

And if your child falters because of evil, then you simply help them turn back to Jesus. Sometimes God gives permission to Satan to really shake us up. Besides the Job instance, another is when Jesus warns Simon Peter:

> "Simon, Simon, Satan has asked to sift all of you as wheat. But I have prayed for you, Simon, that your faith may not fail. And when you have turned back, strengthen your brothers."
> -Luke 22:31-32

This passage refers to Peter's denial of Christ three times the evening before crucifixion. Even with a strong warning from his teacher, Peter is unable to withstand the evil scheme against him. Next time Jesus sees Peter though, Jesus restores their relationship and again calls him to lead others in Christ. In contrast, Judas was provoked by evil to betray Jesus, but without restoration, the progression of sin to shame led Judas to death (Matt. 27).

The discernment of the source of sin mysterious and questionable. Let the Holy Spirit guide your thoughts. Regardless of the cause of sin, the methods you use to help bring your child to restoration with Jesus after falling into sin because of evil are the same.

How may evil be trying to harden you towards God in your emotions, attitudes, or thoughts?

How may evil forces be involved in going after your child's emotions? His attitudes? His thoughts?

Satan has wit and strategy to him. He may see characteristics in your child that if developed will be of mighty use for the Kingdom of God. He often goes after such areas to keep them weak. For example, Peter's strength in the establishment of the church was his boldness for Christ, first seen at Pentecost. When Peter was following Christ, he was often the disciple who said things hastily or argued with Jesus. While immature, Peter's boldness was loud, impetuous, and an area where Satan shook him.

What characteristics does your child have that may be rough around the edges but could be a very strong area God could use to further His Kingdom? Note: to answer this question, you may wish to flip back to character qualities from "You First" section or the "Try it!" worksheet where you summarized your child's attributes.

Take a moment to pray for this quality to be like a seed planted in good soil, that is able to grow and bear much fruit for God (Matthew 13).

Recognition of spiritual warfare brings to the forefront of our minds that this is not a battle against flesh and blood, but against evil. Sometimes in helping your child, it can feel like it is parent versus child. Before picking another battle, take heart: your child, like every person, is under attack. When I think about my child under attack, I prepare to stand firm as a warrior to protect or rescue my baby. This does not necessarily change consequences, but renews commitment and empathy towards my child.

-SIX-
Your Child's Hurts

We have all been hurt. The Bible often refers to hurt as suffering. It is wrongdoing or evil done to you. Uriah's family experienced this hurt when David arranged for his murder, Job at the affliction of disease and great loss, and Jesus by the persecution of religious leaders. The list could go on. Hurt comes in many forms. At the establishment of the church, the apostles regularly admonished the church to do no wrong to one another: In other words, do not hurt each other!

Do not get caught up categorizing your child's hurt in the following questions. Types of hurt overlap. Physical abuse, verbal abuse, inappropriate sexual behavior, and neglect often affect the emotional and physical. Other hurts are primarily physical. For example, Jessica was experiencing bullying at school in the form of physically being pushed around and injured, but her hurt was more emotional due to girls being mean and embarrassing her. I could answer "bullying" in either emotional or physical below and both would be fine. The categories are simply to help provide insight into where your child may be hurt.

What physical hurts has your child experienced in the past?

How has your child dealt with this?

What emotional hurts has your child experienced in the past (i.e. bullying, sibling rivalry, abuse, cruel words)?

How has your child dealt with this?

What hurts has your child experienced due to circumstances like disaster, loss, left out of something significant?

How has your child dealt with this?

Review the disappointments from relationships: Have any of these hurt your child? If so, how?

How has your child dealt with these?

Your child likely has hurts you are unaware of, depending on the personality of the child. If your child communicates verbally, you can ask, " How has anyone hurt you?" or "Can you think of a way someone hurt your feelings recently?" Record their responses here:

Then ask, "What do you think about how they hurt you?" and "How did that make you feel?"

Weariness

"Do not be overcome by evil but overcome evil with good."
--Romans 12:21

When hurts build up, we are susceptible to weariness. It makes sense: we keep trying to do good, but bad things keep coming our way, so we get tired. Weariness can appear as anxiety, falling into temptation frequently, fatigue, quickly becoming upset, becoming unusually quiet, a need to be alone, or insecurity. Weariness over a stressor in your child's life may make all of his daily activities more tiresome. Does your child seem weary? How so?

One remedy for weariness is hope: it develops from perseverance, encouragement, acceptance, and instruction in Truth amidst the trial (Romans 5:3-5). Hope is also a gift from God. If your child seems weary, how can you help bring your child hope?

Another remedy for weariness is doing good, as the verse above states. This concept is similar to that of the Armor of God: when we build up righteousness, it protects us from evil schemes. Doing good through serving others also has an energizing element to it, because we act as vessels for the Holy Spirit to flow through. We get to experience the Holy Spirit when we do good. Considering relationships in your child's life, how can you and your child do good for someone together?

Maybe you are the one that's weary. Parenting a child that is in need of help can feel heavy and lead to weariness. Maybe your child, in his hurt and sin, keeps hurting you, or other relationships in life have led to weariness. Go to the Lord and "Consider Him who ensured such opposition from sinful men so that we will no grow weary and lose heart." (Hebrews 12:3) Spend time focusing on Jesus and all that is bestowed upon you because of His great perseverance. Let Him encourage you and your child.

Parent's Role in Hurt

For better or worse, you have a great deal of influence on your child. You interact with your child more than any other relationship he may have, so the potential for hurts to happen in parent-child relationships is greater than the average relationship. There is no need to deny when we have hurt our children. Instead, own responsibility: confess it to God and your child, seeking forgiveness from both. That discussion can go as simple as, "Ronny, I realized I hurt you earlier today when I yelled at you and rushed you out the door. That was wrong. Will you forgive me?" Is there a wrong you need to address with your child?

Ask your child, "Is there anything I have done that I need to say I am sorry for?" Their perception is true to them. Resist the urge to defend yourself when your child brings up a perceived wrongdoing. Record his reply here:

Besides direct wrongs, parents sometimes place inappropriate demands on children. In our mind, we see what they could do, translate that to what they 'ought' to do, and then demand it (at least in our attitude). Paul speaks to this by saying,

> "Let us therefore make every effort to do what leads to peace and to mutual edification. Do not destroy the work of God for the sake of food." -Romans 14:19

The context of this verse is Paul addressing disputable matters in the church and how some 'mature' believers are trying to force their behaviors on young believers. We do not directly hear how the work of God would be destroyed, but we can infer bitterness, pride, disunity, divisions, discouragement, and insecurity.

As Romans 14 states, we are to make every effort to do what leads to the building up of each other, including children. Often, keeping the peace requires overlooking certain behaviors. Sometimes parents enforce standards with children that are disputable as to whether a behavior is right or wrong. "Disputable matters," as Paul refers to them, are varied and age dependent, but can include food choices, independence in completing chores, friend choice, television shows, word usage, toy preference, and hobby interests. For example, as a foster mom, I had a young boy join our family who cursed often. He also had a lot of behaviors including aggression, running away, and a difficulty speaking English. For weeks, we intentionally overlooked his cursing so he could adjust to our family and work through some of the more important matters. Eventually, his cursing disappeared, and he began mirroring our appropriate language.

How have you been making every effort to do what leads to peace and mutual edification with regard to your child?

Are you arguing over a disputable issue with your child and thus hindering God's work in their lives?

Paul also gives us a method for how to handle disputable issues:
"So whatever you believe about these things keep between yourself and God."
-Romans 14:23

Your child will have issues and preferences that rub you the wrong way. One of the ongoing risks and temptations of Christian parents is legalism. Even what may look like good parenting may not be appropriate or where God is directing you with your child. These are not black-and-white sinful choices, but maybe not the best or wisest behavior according to your interpretation. Consider prayerfully whether it is an area to "keep between yourself and God" for the sake of your child's growth and to deter from the path of legalism. This is why Scripture encourages us to: "Bear with the failings of the weak… Accept one another." (Romans 15:1,7)

What do you need to keep between yourself and Jesus for the sake of peace and mutual edification?

Paul says to "make every effort" to keep unity. What are other efforts you can do to keep peace with your child?

Your Past Hurt

"Do to others what you would have them do to you."
- Luke 6:31

As you prepare to help your child through his hurt, take some time to reflect on how you have been hurt and how others have helped you through your hurt. This will provide a fresh coat of empathy for addressing your child. Most of us have been hurt by others, have self-inflicted hurt, or a circumstance or disaster where we have been hurt. Write about a time in your life you have been hurt:

What sort of behaviors and attitudes did you use to show others you were hurting?

How did others help you through it?

How did God assure you?

What Scriptures come to mind as words that helped you through your time of hurt?

Write about a time you've been weary:

How did you show you were weary?

How did others help you through it?

How did God assure you?

What Scriptures come to mind as especially helpful in your weariness?

Often the most helpful ways others help us through hurts are:

- overlooking our bad attitudes for a time
- meeting our needs
- offering soft assurance or their presence
- encouraging with their words (affirming)
- gone out of their way to pay special attention to how I may perceive the environment (sensitive)
- gentle and kind.
- offering fun to keep our minds from despair
- having open expectations: not surprised at tears for any reason, or tired of company

One Scripture that comes to my mind is Proverbs 16:24:
"Gracious words are a honeycomb, sweet to the soul and healing to the bones."

When you consider what helpful thing others did for you in your hurt, how can you love your child through their hurt?

Humble Helper like Jesus

Read Philippians 2:1-7 and consider the questions below along with this excerpt from those verses.

> "Therefore if you have any encouragement from being united with Christ… then make my joy complete by being like-minded, having the same love, being one in spirit and of one mind. Do nothing out of selfish ambition or vain conceit. Rather, in humility value others above yourselves, not looking to your own interests but each of you to the interests of the others."

Earlier you wrote of encouragement from God during a time of hurt. As such, you qualify as one who has "any encouragement from being united with Christ" (verse 1). Paul is asking you to treat others with the same helpful encouragement you have received. Be like-minded with Christ, have the same love that He does. Be one in His Spirit and His mind. Value what He is doing in your child with your time, energy, and interests. This is the biblical call that comes as a result of being one who has had comfort.

How can you apply these commands as a parenting guide when interacting with your child?

What makes applying these commands to the parent-child relationship difficult?

Ask the Holy Spirit to counsel you. Ask, "God, Am I resisting serving my child in this area?" Read back through Philippians 2:1-7 to spark thought if needed. "Why?"

Ask, "What fears do I have about following these verses in my parenting?"

Ask, "What selfish ambition is getting in the way of my heart's willingness to do this?"

Some days of parenting, I resisted putting a child's interest first. In 'vain conceit' I just wanted the kids to behave well on the outside, even if I was impatiently asking them to shove their hurt away. Other days, I have reasoned, "They need to learn to obey authority" as justification for being a stern leader rather than a comforting servant. More often, the command to put my child's interests first was difficult because I had forgotten how God comforted me. I had forgotten my immaturity and how discouraged I once was.

Spend time in prayer asking God to give you a humble attitude toward your child:

Lord, Thank You for the comfort You've offered me so many times in my life. Thank You for being an approachable Father, who does not turn me away when I fail, but welcomes me with tenderness and speaks right to my hurt. Thank You for allowing me to share in Your Spirit.

Lord, by this Holy Spirit, help me bring compassion, comfort, and tenderness to my child. Empower me to have a humility like Christ so I can show my child Christ in me: to consider my wants and needs and ambitions of no value so that his heart can know You.

Keep me from taking advantage of the position You have given me as a parent. Grant me a willingness to take on child-likeness for the sake of loving this child You have blessed me with. Lord, comfort the hurts impeding my ability to love in this way, and correct wrong ways of thinking in me that justify disobeying Your Word.

Feel free to write out a personal prayer here as well:

Promises

> "Not one of all the Lord's good promises to Israel failed; every one was fulfilled."
> -Joshua 21:45

Part of God's nature is that of a promise keeper. Throughout the Bible, God lavishes His people with promises through prophets, angels, and His own voice. Then, He fulfills what He said He would do. Trust and hope result. For example, consider these responses to God fulfilling His promises:

> Praise be to the LORD, who has given rest to his people Israel just as he promised. Not one word has failed of all the good promises he gave through his servant Moses. May the LORD our God be with us as he was with our fathers; may he never leave us nor forsake us. May he turn our hearts to him, to walk in all his ways and to keep the commands, decrees and regulations he gave our fathers.
> —1 Kings 8:56-58

How did the people respond to a fulfilled promise?

In another Scripture, the Psalmist declares amidst a weary, depressing time:
> "Your promises have been thoroughly tested, and your servant loves them."
> -Psalm 119:40

What strikes you about this verse?

Hurt breeds distrust, not only to the one responsible for the hurt but with many other relationships as well. For example, if Seth is abused by an uncle, he may be distrustful of men in general. When a child is hurt by any adult, whether a teacher, relative or a stranger, he may be distrustful towards parents.

Lack of trust commonly leads to sin, especially in the parent child relationship. Parents are a child's main authority, so if children do not trust authority, all sorts of wrongdoing at home, school, and society can be expected. We do the same with God: when we do not trust in God's goodness, we seek 'goodness' in other places and on our terms.

Therefore we can learn to rebuild trust by how God does it with His children. God rebuilds and reaffirms Himself to His children by:
> 1. providing promises and keeping them
> 2. teaching them about God's promises and how He has met them.

God provides and teaches promises through words, love, and modeling. To be a Christian parent is to parent in the same nature God does. So, consider how you can do the same.

What are some promises you have made to your children? These can be ordinary, every-day type of commitments. You do not need to have said, "I promise I will…" or "I swear I will…" Saying you will do something is a promise ((Matthew 5: 37).

1.

2.

3.

Have you fulfilled them?

If not, seek your child's forgiveness. A failure to follow through is a sin (Matthew 5:33-37). If you have been faithful to fulfill your word, remind your child in a humble tone, as if a reaffirmation of your love for them. This may sound like sharing a thought, "Remember how I told you we would get to play on the trampoline together and then I chased you to it right when we got home from the trip last week!"

What can you do to fulfill any promises you have already made?

Think about something you are planning to do for your child this week. It does not need to be fancy. Children generally thrive under structure or routine. Promises are a form of structure, where children can expect a certain thing to happen. For example, "I am planning on reading a story each night to my child this week." The plan does not have to be new. It can be something you have been doing, or something you know they need. Write one, or a few intentions:

Share these plans with your child. Say, "Honey, tonight when it's time for bed, we are going to have a special time together. I am going to cuddle up with you and I am going to read you a story." You may see your child light up, hope for it, and remind you throughout the day or at night time. Or, your child may not respond at all, nor say a word about it. He is waiting to see if you will do as you say. He is testing you. So, be like God to His children and do what you say you will do.

The more this happens, the more trust will build, and the more your child will grow out of their hurt. The same healthy development happens with infants. They cry out in need, parents meet the need. Trust grows. Somewhere along the line your child may have lost trust. It may have been no fault of your own. If you have determined your child is hurt, give consistent and frequent love and hope by fulfilling promises.

A Note on Jesus' Hurt

Though Jesus was without sin, He was hurt. He suffered both the physical torture and crucifixion as well as the emotional pain of wrongful accusations and humiliating death. Read John 20:24-27. When Jesus appeared to the disciples after his resurrection from the dead, He had nail marks from those who hurt Him. God does not assure us the marks of hurt will go away. Even Jesus carried deep scars. But God does assure us the pain can be transformed.

What are some reasons God may allow scars remain (thoughts and/or Scripture)?

> "Not only so, but we also glory in our sufferings, because we know that suffering produces perseverance; perseverance, character; and character, hope."
> -Romans 5:3-4

Our child's wounds may be life long, and scars may remain. But the pain can, and should, subside when the Holy Spirit works in their heart to bring character, hope, and understanding.

Addressing Hurt

The goal in addressing your child's hurt is healing it as completely as possible. This will restore a base of trust and right perspective. You can help through prayer, play, and promises. Healing happens with nurturing, some correction, and time. Jot a few ideas you have about what this would look like for you and your child.

Six: Your Child's Hurts

How can you pray about your child's hurts?

What promises of God can you share with your child? For example, a song I consistently sing during night terrors is, "When I am afraid I will trust in you, in God whose name I praise." -Psalm 56:3

What promises can you offer to your child?

Ask God for a Scriptural promise for your child. In the next few days as you come to the Word, be looking for what God is planning for your child.

Nurturing is a means of providing assurance. Humans build trust through physical touch. Activities like hugs, applying lotion, brushing hair, cuddling, making eye contact when speaking, hand holding, positive body-language, laughing, time or games together all can provide assurance. How can you nurture your child?

Write a few from the list on the "Try it!" worksheet.

When a child is hurt or being corrected, he is especially vulnerable. Use careful wording and continue to pour on the love through nurturing. As you move on to the next section, nurture in exceedingly higher proportions than correction.

-SEVEN-
Your Child's Sins

Besides hurts, your child may have sins in his life causing issues. Before addressing your child's sin(s) specifically, take some time to study the pattern of sin in general, as well as some biblical codes for changing habitual sins.

Pattern of sin

Read Joshua chapter 7, and as you do so look for a pattern, or progression of sin. After you have read the text, take a closer look at a couple verses, 19-20:

> "Then Joshua said to Achan, "My son, give glory to the Lord, the God of Israel, and honor him. Tell me what you have done; do not hide it from me. Achan replied, "It is true! I have sinned against the Lord, the God of Israel. This is what I have done: When I saw in the plunder a beautiful robe from Babylonia, two hundred shekels of silver and a bar of gold weighing fifty shekels, I coveted them and took them. They are hidden in the ground inside my tent, with the silver underneath."

Achan gives an insightful account of what was going on in his head and heart, and how he sinned against the God of Israel. Fill in the blanks:

When I _____ in the plunder a beautiful robe...

I _____ them and _____ them.

They are _____ in the ground inside my tent.

The progression of sin can be observed through many other biblical accounts too, such as David committing adultery, Cain murdering Abel, Eve eating of the fruit, and even in the manner Satan tempts Jesus in the wilderness. The four words you filled in from the passage form a common pattern: from observing to coveting to taking to hiding.

Now, consider the issues you identified for your child as areas in need of help. Is your child in any of the four progressions of sin right now with regards to that issue:

If so, what are they observing?

What are they coveting?

What are they taking?

What are they hiding?

Historically, soldiers commonly took plunder when they conquer a city. This was an a cultural expectation. Their bounty seen as part of their compensation and reward. Achan may have justified his sin because it was normal. Likewise, many sins are justifiable, but that does not make them right. What did Achan do that he should not have done, which made his actions sinful? (You will have to look earlier in Joshua)

If you wrote down a sin you observed your child considering/doing: is this something they justify culturally? If your child is openly and consistently in a certain pattern of sin, ask your child genuinely, "How come you think this behavior is acceptable?"

Why is it wrong?

Does your child know it's wrong?

SEVEN: YOUR CHILD'S SINS

...e this cycle repeating itself in your ... statement similar to the one below as ...e cycle of sin? For example: When I see ...em and take them. I hide them in my ...y came in to ...ty was

In the sample statement above the child may have been motivated by recognition, or maybe he was promised video game time as a reward for good grades. Eve was motivated to eat the fruit in the Garden of Eden by the promise of knowledge and being like God (Genesis 3). So sometimes the thing we covet has an underlying motive. What motivation does your child have for his desire to sin?

Back up and consider how Joshua draws this confession out of Achan. First, Joshua is confused and troubled by Isreal's defeat. Secondly, Joshua seeks the Lord asking, "Why?!" Then, God provides the answer of sin and the person responsible. Next, Joshua addresses Achan. With what type of attitude do you perceive Joshua addressing Achan?

Parents can follow a similar model in leading to get to the bottom of confusing troublesome matters:

1. Seek God asking "Why?" and look for His provision of direction and understanding.

2. If God directs you toward a sin in your child, give him an opportunity to share. You can do this by questioning in a gentle, but firm manner that exposes their sin is against the Lord, and explaining that they can honor God by taking their sin out of hiding.

3. Let your child verbalize their sin to hear themselves say it. Confession holds a freeing power.

4. Provide discipline.

Look back at Joshua 7. You may be struck by the result of Achan's sin. Even after confessing, he is stoned. Just in case you interpret this passage literally, hear this advice: do not stone your child!

> "The blood of Jesus, his Son, purifies us from all sin... If we confess our sins, He is faithful and just and will forgive us our sins and purify us from all unrighteousness."
> -1 John 1:9

Praise be to God we are living post-resurrection, where God forgives our sins through Jesus Christ's sacrifice on the cross. When your child is drawn to confess to you, lead them to confess and seek forgiveness from God and those they have offended. Help them understand the grace of God in Christ Jesus. Discipline can be helpful to lead them toward this repentance as well as encourage future obedience.

Does your child have an age-appropriate understanding of forgiveness of their sins only through Jesus Christ?

How can you tell?

If your child is grasping the grace of God through Jesus Christ, their chains of sin are broken and they have been set free. You are here to help them walk in their freedom, and we will look at ways to do this shortly.

If you are not confident they understand Jesus Christ as Savior, start there. Continue to explain and model nurturing, discipline, and forgiveness. This routine, along with biblical teaching, will lead to understanding by the Grace of God. You cannot expect your child to conquer sin without the Holy Spirit.

Read Romans 6-8 for a clearer understanding on the role of the Holy Spirit and sin.

Cracking the code

Like a virus in a computer, sin follows a certain pattern to destroy us. Breaking those patterns requires intentional re-programming. The Bible provides us with such codes, or keys.

We have a sinful nature at work in us like a virus. Just like Achan justified taking the robe and money as plunder, we all at some point justify our sin in our thoughts based upon our desires. These thoughts are birthed out of a sinful nature hostile toward God.

So, conquering sin is to squelch the sinful nature in us that is hostile toward God. Thankfully, by the grace of Jesus Christ, this can be done. If you did not read Romans 6-8 in the previous section on your child's sin, do so now. Some of the following terminology will be understood in the fuller context of those chapters.

The question to ask as parents, then, is how does one crack the sinful nature? Paul provides insight:

> "Therefore, I urge you brothers and sisters, in view of God's mercy, to offer your bodies as a living sacrifice, holy and pleasing to God--this is your true and proper worship. Do not conform to the pattern of this world, but be transformed by the renewing of your mind. Then you will be able to test and approve what God's will is—His good, pleasing, and perfect will."
> -Romans 12:1-2

This passage in Romans has a key. Earlier in Romans, Paul explained that when ruled by the sinful nature, we do not think God's will is good. Therefore we go against God's will when we feel like it (also known as sinning). To turn this corrupted thinking and acting around takes God's mercy. He offers us the choice to let His Holy Spirit come in and help us. Therefore, he urges us to: (Fill in the blanks on the instructions given from the verses above.)

1. _____ __ _____ as a living sacrifice

2. _____ __ _____ to the pattern of this world, but

3. ___ _____ by the renewing of your mind.

Along with instructions are motivations. An understanding of the mercy of God motivates us to offer our bodies as sacrifices and not conform to worldly patterns. When we know He is God and calls us to live perfectly, we rely upon Him in recognition we cannot succeed on our own.

To be a Christian is to believe God has taken away His wrath towards us, through Jesus Christ's sacrifice. We deserve death, but He gives us life instead. This is mercy, and an understanding of mercy precedes one's willingness to live differently than the world.

Besides instructions and motivations, this passage shares what the results of following through will be. If I decide my body and life is the Lord's, resist the pattern of this world, and renew my mind with Truth, I will approve of God's will. When I approve of God's will, I will follow God's will. Since people typically do what they think is right, it makes sense why this formula breaks the power of sin. Living out the spiritual nature (sacrifice, transformation, renewal) squelches our sinful nature. We start to want righteousness. God's way starts to feel like common sense, or at least good and pleasing, and the sinful nature starts to seem displeasing.

The trick to this key is analogous to a heavy wheel. To get started takes a big push, but then when its moving, the weight feeds the momentum. Most people find sacrifice and breaking away from the pattern of this world to be really hard and your child will too. But, once we see how good, pleasing, and perfect God's will is, then the Truth will help make other areas of breaking away from sin easier.

As a parent, you get to give your child a push-start by providing examples, encouragement, discipline, rewards, and fun to lighten the load. Any area of obedience to what the Lord is asking of you, in Scripture or through other revelation, is a way you can offer yourself as a living sacrifice. With that in mind:

What are some ways may God be leading you to offer your body as a living sacrifice?

What ways may God be directing your child to offer his body as a living sacrifice?

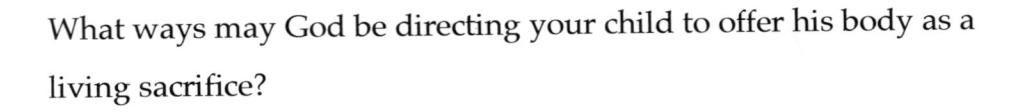

What are ways you can renew your mind?

Which of these ways can your child renew his mind?

> "That, however, is not the way of life you learned when you heard about Christ and were taught in him in accordance with the truth that is in Jesus. You were taught, with regard to your former way of life, to put off your old self, which is being corrupted by its deceitful desires; to be made new in the attitude of your minds; and to put on the new self, created to be like God in true righteousness and holiness."
> -Ephesians 4:20-24

Paul says when Christians heard about Christ they were taught a three part formula:

1. Take former way of life and put it off (sin).

SEVEN: YOUR CHILD'S SINS

2. Be made new in the attitude (transformed thinking).
3. Put on a new self (character and righteous behavior).

Take a deeper look into the passage above: What reason does the passage give for putting off the former way of life?

What are some other words for deceit?

What are some other words for desire?

We have already discussed how your child may have desires that are off-base because of false expectations or selfishness. These thoughts lead to a corruption, which creates all sorts of sinful ways of life. This could be the undercurrent of some of your child's issues. This formula in Ephesians 4 might fit your child in some way if he is caught up in sin.

A lot of therapeutic and parenting advice hits part of the Ephesians 4 formula. Trying to discipline bad behavior out of a child is tempting. "If he goes to time-out often enough for hitting, he will learn." Or, to positively reinforce good behavior: "If we just praise her for sharing, she will eventually stop snatching from others." These methods can work for a time because they are tapping into what is true, but a full measure of truth is needed for lasting change and growth.

So besides taking off the 'old self,' people are instructed to "be made new in the attitude of your minds." How do you think this passage could relate to Romans 12:1-2 from a few pages back?

Now consider "putting on a new self." What description does the passage give about the new self?

The new self is not just behavioral change; rather it's a new direction in the pursuit of righteousness and holiness. The person, character and being, is changed.

This formula for change is not necessarily a sequential process, although it can be. Sometimes, it happens all at once. To gain a better grasp of the concept, Paul gives some examples of putting on a new self in the rest of chapter four. Use the chart on the following page while reading through verses 25-32:

Put off old self	New attitude of mind	Put on new self
ex: falsehood	we are all one body (Therefore lying to others is misleading the whole church)	speak truthfully

Besides the examples listed in Ephesians 4, what are some examples you could fill in what it means to: put off, new attitude, put on? Add them in the chart above. These do not need to be specific for your child.

Paul's formula for change is a valuable principle, and its

success is based on a person's knowledge and discipline through the Holy Spirit. By the time your child is an adult, a reasonable goal is maturity in his faith so that he puts on his new self. One role in parenting is to train him to get to that point.

One time I had little children ages four, three, toddler, and infant. In the morning, the eldest two went to pre-school, so having everyone fed, dressed and out the door by eight was my daily morning challenge. I laid out clothes for the three year old boy Oscar and dressed his baby brother there in the room so Oscar would stay focused and put his clothes on. Then, I chased down my toddler with clothes in hand and helped dress her where I found her, saying things like, "Alright, now push your arm through." Somewhere in the midst, my princess pre-schooler came down in a dress and likely some mismatch. Most days, the outfit was good to go and I told her she looked beautiful. Other times, I coaxed her to change the outfit, sometimes a tantrum, and others with smiling compliance.

Just as children have physical ages that require age-appropriate treatment and help, our children are in spiritual stages that require various stages of help. We spend at least a couple years dressing a child before he can be expected to dress himself. Then he still needs oversight to stay focused. Eventually, he just needs encouragement and correction.

This translates spiritually into:

- **Putting off old: boundaries, discipline, logical**

> consequences, withdrawing temptation, re-direction
>
> - **New attitude: teaching, spiritual disciplines**
> - **Put on new: role modeling, training, practicing, praising**

On special occasions, I still lay out clothes for my kids (and even my husband). Some occasions, even after your child typically has the character to live righteously in an area, require special help and training to prepare them. For example, I would not allow my thirteen year old boy to go to a certain friend's house. This was a boundary I set up because I saw them interact together and knew he did not have the discernment or self-control to steer clear of sin without my oversight. Sometimes when that boy was over I provided activities like a cooler of water balloons for them to fill up and play with, because I knew their own ideas would not be appropriate.

Addressing Specific Sins

Now, before we move on to more specific ways to help, apply the Ephesians 4 formula to your child. Look at the Roots chart at each column with "sin involved" filled in. The sin is the "old self" ways we are looking to help him put off. Next would be a new attitude of mind. Considering Romans 12, think of a truth in the Bible related to an area of struggle with sin. This can be a specific command against the sin or an encouragement to do the new behavior. Think of any Scripture that would help your child understand God's mercy or break the pattern he is currently following. For help on finding specific verses, see "How to find out what the Bible has to say about a certain issue" in the Appendix. Place the reference in the chart, but write out the whole verses below.

Remember, this process only works to the degree your child knows the grace of God through Jesus Christ. There is a fine line on the surface between training for goodness sake or for growth in character, but in the heart it is a great divide. The difference is that of the Law and the Gospel. Take a minute to read the following in prayer:

Holy Spirit, on You alone can I depend. I know that unless I build upon the foundation You have set in my child's life, I work in vain. I recognize that as parent I am a vessel for Your love and purposes for my child. Keep this on the forefront of my mind, because sometimes I get caught up in trying to manipulate my child into conformity so it is easy for me or so I look good as a parent. As I ask for Your help in helping my child I recognize that You are at work in greater measures than anything I could do. Keep me focused on my child's heart and provide divine discernment to be able to see where my child is living under the Law of sin and death as well as rejoice where his heart is following You and Your righteousness.

SEVEN: YOUR CHILD'S SINS

Amen.

Children gain self-control over temptation when they understand cause and effect. Both the negative effects of the sin as well as the positive effects of righteous behavior provide motivation. For example, Paul uses effects to motivate when in Ephesians 4 he says people who work hard will have money to spare.

Make a list of the possible effects of you child's current sinful behavior:

How can you demonstrate to him these risks/effects?

Make a list of the possible effects of the desired 'new self' behavior:

How can you demonstrate to your child these effects?

How do you see the desired new attitude, behavior, or character portrayed in your child's world already: in every day activities, relationships, or certain life situations? For example, if the new self is respecting elders, maybe a character in your child's favored comic respects his teacher well. This may be tricky to answer right away. Carefully think about it and pray for God to help reveal correlations this week.

What ways can you incorporate these correlations from their interests into intentional learning? Write any ideas on the 'Try it!' Page from the appendix. (More to come on this soon. If you are stumped here, that is alright, just move on.)

Discipline

You may be wondering, "So where does discipline come in?" Your child may very well need discipline to facilitate taking off his old self, being made new in his attitude of mind, not conforming to the world, and/or putting on his new self. Discipline is a tool for forming your child into the wholeness God designed him for. By-products of parental discipline may be morality or convenience, but those perks are not the purpose. Discipline is for the purpose of becoming like Christ (Hebrews 12), and this truth should be on the fore front of your mind with regards to discipline.

In your child's journey of sanctification, he will often need firm guidance through such things as rules, boundaries, and consequences. As he matures toward adulthood, a shift towards self-discipline and forming his own accountability should happen. This is not a book about specific ways to bring about consequences to your child nor a manual for godly independence, but since discipline overlaps helping, a few principles are note worthy:

Let the Holy Spirit be your guide to methods (John 14-17). Although thousands of parenting books tell you the "right way" to discipline, Jesus intentionally leaves parenting methods open. He has an individual plan and purpose for His (your) child. Each child will serve a unique purpose which will require varying preparations. He knew creating a parenting manual made no sense. So instead He gave us each an individual parenting coach (also known as the Holy Spirit). Listen to Him!

Here are some principles on godly discipline from Hebrews 12:1-17, which I recommend reading. The teaching is preceded by a chapter on faith. Faith comes before training in righteousness:

A. Discipline will be hard for you and the child. God works

mutually and as you endure the hardship of consistently training your child, God is disciplining you too, so do not give up (Verses 1-11).

B. When under discipline, people can lose heart easily. Therefore, remind your child when disciplining them of your love and acceptance of him (Verses 5-6).

C. Everyone must undergo discipline (Verses 7-8).

D. Your child will respect you for disciplining them, after "a little while" (Which may be referring to adulthood!) (Verse 9).

E. The purpose of discipline is holiness (Verse 10-11).

F. Consider, is your method of discipline strengthening your child to prepare a smoother future for him and others, or is it breaking him down (Verses 12-13)?

G. If you discipline when you are not living in peace with your child nor being holy in your conduct and attitude, then your child will not see the Lord in it (Verse 14).

H. Be very careful your discipline leads to the grace of God, and no bitterness starts growing in your child, or it will "cause trouble and defile many" (Verse 15).

I. Ensure your child comprehends and values the magnificent inheritance he has as a child of God, so he does not see it lightly and thus treat it poorly. Esau did this by selling his inheritance for a cup of soup (verses 16-17).

Let these principles guide you as you develop disciplinary practices for your child.

-EIGHT-
Putting the Pieces Together

One at a time

Sometimes awareness helps trigger enough growth to conquer whatever issue your child faces. Thinking about your child, his relationships, his hurts, and his sins may have surfaced the issue enough so that you see the way to move forward. Or maybe you have realized his expressions are typical for his age and God will give you the grace to bear with it while he grows. However, bringing this awareness to your child is likely part of the growth God intends. This chapter considers how to impart the knowledge you have to your child in a loving manner:

> "Knowledge puffs up while love builds up."
> -1 Corinthians 8:1b

We now have a couple of handfuls of knowledge to juggle in a manner that will build up your child. In one hand, we know about your child: his unique considerations, his spirituality, his relationships, his hurt, his sin. In the other hand is knowledge of how to deal with spiritual growth, hurt, and sin from the Bible. Now begins the juggle.

At this point, we are going to identify and focus on one issue.

Look at the Roots chart and choose a problem to tackle first. Choose an issue which is big enough to matter but simple enough to try first. For example, a daughter's bulimic disorder is important, but may be involved in a complicated cycle along with several relationships, expectations, idols, etc. If I address her arguing first, which I charted to be based off of a main hurt, then her load will be lightened and we will have an easier time in the future conquering bulimic behaviors.

The Bible directly warns against trying to mold your child too much at once. It is called exasperation (Ephesians 6:4, Colossians 3:21). My prayer is for the Holy Spirit to give you the self-control, gentleness, patience, grace, mercy, and peace to bear with the other problems well, while you focus on one.

Which issue are you moving forward with first:

You may have already written out insights about this issue in previous sections and in the Roots chart. Below you will look at it cyclically to bring more understanding. Sometimes determining whether sins, hurts, or beliefs came first is difficult. To illustrate the difficulty of determining the source, I have placed an example of the various factors in the cycle below.

EIGHT: PUTTING THE PIECES TOGETHER

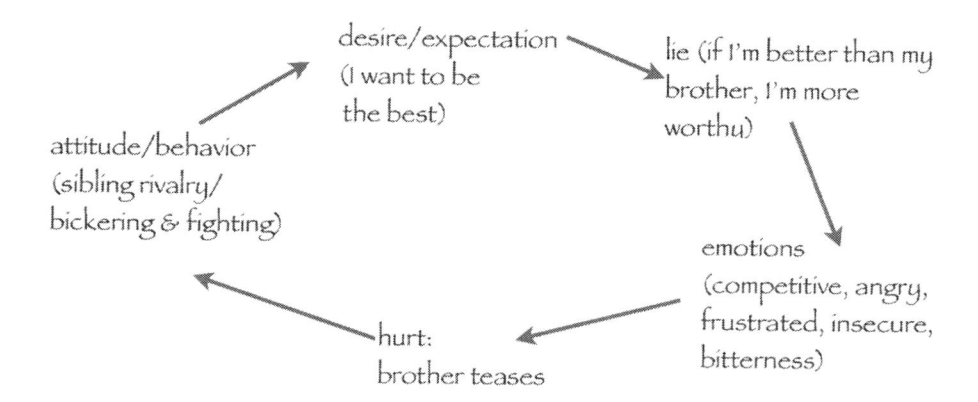

desire/expectation (I want to be the best) → **lie** (if I'm better than my brother, I'm more worthy) → **emotions** (competitive, angry, frustrated, insecure, bitterness) → **hurt:** brother teases → **attitude/behavior** (sibling rivalry/ bickering & fighting) → (back to desire/expectation)

Try drawing out a cycle of the first issue you plan on approaching, by using your chart and summary.

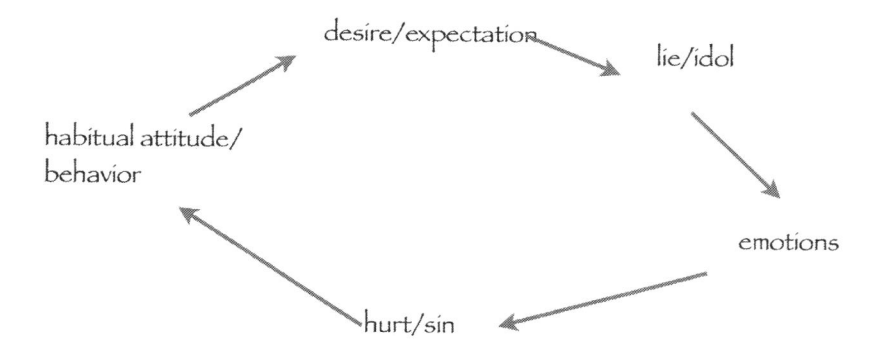

desire/expectation → **lie/idol** → **emotions** → **hurt/sin** → **habitual attitude/behavior** → (back to desire/expectation)

Write out a sentence summary of the cycle at work within your child.

125

Our Great Example

Consider how Jesus imparts knowledge of the Kingdom of God: The first part of the book of Matthew records Jesus' growth and establishment of ministry. Next, He performs several miracles and gathers followers to Himself, teaching many. Then, what does Jesus ask of the disciples in Matthew 10:1-8?

After going out to practice what Jesus modeled, the disciples returned and Jesus continues teaching them through example and instruction.
Read Matthew 13:24-35. How does Jesus frame deep truth for the disciples?

As Jesus personally grew he taught, modeled, had disciples practice, and explained deep truths in the context of the things they understood through analogies, parables, and stories. Throughout all of this, Jesus encouraged them. Therefore, as a parent do as Jesus did: personally grow, teach your children, model to them, give them opportunity to practice, and make truth understandable.

As a Child

By now you should have a better grasp on the complexities of your child. Hopefully, you have identified a problem and a solution, whether in regards to hurt or sin. Maybe dwelling on your child has provided the knowledge and energy needed to help your child already. Maybe your child just needed some validation that you recognize his hardship. Maybe you have realized that the troubles lie within you. Odds are your child still needs to understand the biblical principles in a context which makes sense to him, which is likely through play.

Translating truths it into the context of play is as essential as Jesus giving His disciples opportunities to practice. Different forms of play offer ways to practice skills of life. Playing can be crafts, games, activities, role playing, or musical. Play can be as individual or group, imaginative or structured. Words and teaching about the issue surely can be incorporated, but playing is the main medium.

Using gentleness with your child helps address the sinful nature but keeps your child's Spirit encouraged. Direct truth and correction through words can be traumatic or confusing. Framing concepts in contexts children understand brings greater understanding than pure vocabulary. Remember, one of the goals is for your child to be able to 'dress himself' with new righteousness. This takes coaching and practice.

Look back at your child's skills and learning summary on the

"Try it!" page in the appendix. As you do so, ask the Holy Spirit: *How can this information about my child be used to help him understand the Word of God he needs for this issue?* Keep an open mind for ideas. You may find scanning the whole section on Taking a Look at Your Child helpful as well. Keep the "Try it!" page handy.

You and your child can come together to play, or you can use play as the means to counsel. We are looking for play that provides an opportunity to respond and engage. This can look like:

A. Accepting your leadership (love, touch, invitation to engage, encouragement, identifying).

B. Mirroring what you are teaching by doing (modeling, reciprocating, learning).

C. Practicing living out of truth in their attitudes and behaviors (training).

When you consider your child's current hurt and sin, which purpose for play is most applicable? If all apply, rank them in order of strongest need.

As you look at these key factors, did the Holy Spirit reveal any ideas of how to incorporate the Truth into play? Write a few ideas you have on the "Try it!" page before looking at the list of ideas provided below.

Ways to Play

Considering the specific truth you are seeking to impart, look at the list of ideas below and choose several activities that can be adapted for the purpose your child needs, matched with the way your child grows. Write three of them on the "Try it!" page. Look at the "Try it! Example" page as well to see how I related the ways of playing to a specific case.

Most activities serve more than one purpose, but I categorized them by primary purpose. This is obviously not an exhaustive list, but will spark some ideas to get you going.

Accepting
- Role playing: Using your child's preferred toy (cars, action figures, dolls, play house/school), let your child act out any emotion without judgement. Respond with toys in gentleness and love, identifying verbally for them what they're acting out. For example, if child is bullying: "Little train, you sure are acting mean to the others by bumping into them. You are angry, but I'll still be your friend. Let's race over here."
- Use musical forms like dance, karaoke, musical chairs, make up music, jam. Use utensils in the kitchen to create instruments. Learn a song together. Make up a dance to a

song, especially one that incorporates Scripture.
- Break a dish, toy, photo and make into a mosaic
- Drawing inside-out: trace each others hands. Outside the hand draw a picture of what feelings you're showing to others, and inside the hand those feelings you have inside.
- Have a "video contest" to find a short internet video that best shows the truth.
- Each create a word scramble with key words related to the truth. Then you swap and solve the puzzles

Mirroring
- Keep a pen-pal journal with you and your child. In it write notes of affirmation, ask silly or serious questions, and draw pictures for him. Using a diary with a lock can be extra special.
- Use balls to roll, catch, hide and find; play hot potato
- Mime each other. For example, make an angry face. Have them make an angry face. Say, "Oh yeah, good angry face." Then make a surprised face. Have them make a surprised face. Affirm: "Good surprised face!" And continue with other emotions.
- Play observation games such as, "I spy," "Guess Who," or "Twenty-questions."
- Video games. Swap controllers half way through playing a race/game iteration.

- Water games like water balloon toss, blowing bubbles, or running through a sprinkler.

Practice
- Role playing: using your child's preferred toy, provoke the situation for your child to respond correctly. For example, let child pretend to be mommy doll, and you the sisters. Have your big sister doll hit the baby doll, and let your child mommy correct and discipline the sister.
- Play emotional charades where you and your child pick out written emotions and act them out.
- Take turns acting out scenes from a common show or story that relate to their issues.
- Let your child choose a board game to play. Interactions of competition or cooperation may challenge your child.
- Paint emotions. For example, draw a picture of people, houses, animals and weather. Have your child label the picture. Or, have your child draw what makes him mad using only the color red. Now go back and add blue for sad, and orange for happy.
- "Interview" strangers in a store or waiting room together with a made-up survey question.
- Let your child publish a family newspaper, with few guidelines. You will see the family from their lens.

Back to the Parent

Throughout this book you recorded several aspects about your relationship with your child. What are the areas you are working on as a parent that will help your child? (You may need to review "Using This Workbook," "You First," or "Taking a Look at your Child's Relationships" shapes).

Spend a minute to pray for God to work in these areas of parenting.

Sometimes to focus on one area will require leniency in another areas. For example, when I concentrated on activities to help my little girl deal with an attachment disorder, we took a break from potty training. Or, on a smaller scale, when I worked on diligence with homework with my teenager, I became lenient on his after-dinner responsibilities. Are there any areas you can overlook while a different correction is in focus?

If your child resists playing with you

Although you now have ideas of new things to try with your child, he may reject you. This can be disheartening, but keep a few things in mind to build your relationship into welcoming intimacy.

- Be respectful of his time. Maybe you have not given him enough notice and he is involved with something else, or tired. When he say "no," first try to encourage a "This will be fun." Or "do you have something you'd rather do with me?" Let him choose the first few days worth of activities. Your turn will come.

- Lighten the directness. Your child may resist your efforts because of fear. Try going less direct by incorporating the play into a normal activity like dinner preparations or driving. Or, gather group involvement by inviting a couple of your child's friends or siblings into the activity. For one of my foster children, hugging and eye-contact was too direct, but he would let me wash his hands and wipe his face after meals.

- Offer more opportunities to play. If your child is not accustomed to your being playful, the first few invitations may seem strange or like you are up to something (which you are!).

- Ask the Holy Spirit what you can do.

- Consider if your child needs to hear an apology or affirmation from you, or if there is another barrier between you and your child.

- You may be asking too much of your child at this point. You may think it's light, but to your child what you are asking is too difficult. Try providing easier alternatives.

Tips on playing

Just as education accumulates over time, training in righteousness is not a one-time-shot. Helping a child through hurts and sins may take more time than you would like. In the meantime:

- Relax and enjoy your child (even if he does not seem to be doing likewise).

- Celebrate milestones. Focus on and reward good behaviors or achievements.

- Even all-stars flop. If your idea or its facilitation does not seem to work, just try a different type.

- Show mercy. Your child is not perfect either.

Furthermore, your child needs affirmation: just as a good coach gives a pep talk to his team, for every word of correction you give include plenty of praise and affirmation. Three to seven times as much is what the pros recommend, but don't let that ratio discourage you! Circle ideas to affirm below you can do this week. You can repeat the same things over and over again, and it wouldn't be overkill.

- "I'm so proud of you for…"
- Give a hug and kiss. Say, "I love you" often.
- Praise an unrelated area: "Wow Josh, you've been really helpful with your sister this week when you…"
- Solicit praise from others. Email his teacher to ask for something he's been doing well. Then say, "I heard from Mrs. Smith you have been turning in your homework early all week! Keep it up buddy!"
- "Wow! Look at all you've done!"
- Thank them for helping with dinner.
- "I noticed today…(something she did that showed character)."
- Compare to how she's grown from the past

Goal Setting

Tools are worthless unless they are put into good use. You have thought about helping your child, and have been equipped with some useful tools, so now help them! Remember to focus doubly on helping your child respond to the issue, as well as instilling hope for his growth. Commit to 15 minutes of intentional 'counseling' play with your child three days a week. Or, set your own reasonable time goal. How can you make these a priority in your life and parenting?

If you have identified multiple issues for your child, create a longer term plan by using the table in the appendix. By laying out how and when you will address each issue, you will gain greater patience and hope in the plan. It will allow you to overlook issues for a season, knowing you will get to them soon. Even if you just want to fill in the top row identifying the issue now, you can come back to fill in the rest of the plan as that time approaches. Move onto the next issue when you see your child growing in his comfort level with applying truth with regards to the current issue. As you transition to focusing on the next thing, make sure to come back to some play or talk about previous truths so they become habitual.

Thanksgiving

We have a tendency to forget how far we have come. Reflect in prayer for a few minutes and ask God, "What has my child conquered?"

Take some time to say or write a prayer of thanksgiving to God for how He has worked in your child in these areas.

Look back at the list of character qualities from the You First chapter. How have you or your child developed in character since you started the workbook? Thank God for it specifically.

As you come to the Word in the next week or so ask, "Is there anything else You'd like me to know about my child right now?"

Journaling

As you enact these biblical principles in word and play, keep a record of what has been successful, what has not worked so well, and how your child has grown. A template with questions in the appendix will help you journal.

A Final Prayer

Lord, bless these parents for their heart to please You and bring Your glory onto the earth. Thank You for blessing them with children, and using children to give them the opportunity to be like You. Thank You for Your perfect parenting, and helping us continually. May You provide that same divine patience and discernment to empathize, assist, and encourage these readers. This small endeavor we recognize as part of Jesus's Great Commission, and trust that in teaching children to follow You, You will be with us. We take great comfort and authority in Your indwelling presence, and listen for Your guidance. Thank You. Amen.

Appendix

How to find out what the Bible has to say about a certain issue.

1. Be in the Word as often as possible, at least daily, with attentive reading, studies of characters or attributes. If you want to be a strong Christian parent a competent knowledge and application of the Word of God is essential. This comes by diligence and practice. Often in a topic of conversation, we think, "Oh yeah, I just saw something about that in the news." or "Jane and I were just talking about that." Scripture will be the same way if we are in it and talking about it.

2. Do a keyword search through either websites like www.biblegateway.com or www.blueletterbible.org, software like eSword, printed concordance books, or topical reference books like <u>For Instruction in Righteousness</u> (By Pam Forster), <u>Quick Scripture Reference for Counseling</u> (By John Kruis), or <u>Praying God's Word</u> (By Beth Moore).

3. Cross-reference. When looking at one verse, ask yourself, "Can I think of any story in the Bible that speaks to this?" Or, "Where else does the Bible talk about this?" Some Bibles have a cross-reference list in the center margin that contain related verses, and many websites offer the same tool.

4. Many people are encouraged by Christian music. If a certain song speaks to an issue, look at the lyrics on the artist's website or in search engines and see if they are based on Scripture.

5. Ask someone. Many pastors, Sunday-school teachers, or Christian friends would be glad to help.

Relationship: _____ to _____

Trust

Obey

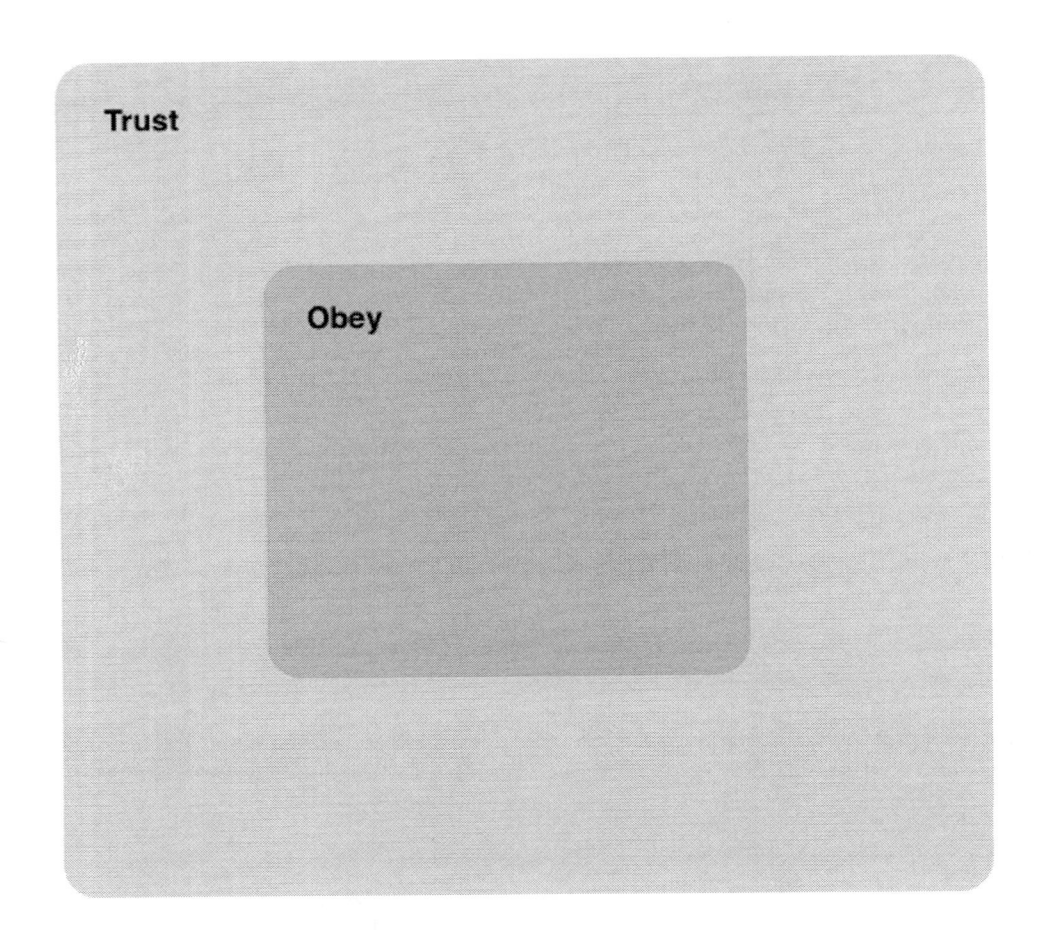

Roots Chart

Each column represents a seemingly separate issue. Some rows and columns may be left blank if not applicable. See sample chart on the following pages.

Issue				
Disappointment				
Emotion				
Expectation				
Origin of Expectation				
Related lies				
Idols involved				

Appendix

Hurt			
Sin involved			
"New attitude of mind" / Truth			
"New self"			
Armor of God for situation			

Roots Chart
EXAMPLE

Issue	Snatching	Yelling at little sister	Tantrums after school
Disappointment	"I'm not getting what I want"	Tension with dad, sister annoys	School was hard
Emotion	Impatient, angry	Annoyed, sad, confused, frustrated	Exhausted, confused
Expectation	Play and do what I want	I'd be living with dad by now	It'll be fun and go by without challenge
Origin of Expectation	Mostly he does play and do what he wants	Dad promised	Other kids are having fun and doing well
Related lies	My want trumps their want	I'm not worth anything	I should perform like everybody else
Idols involved	self	Dad?	

Hurt		Dad broke promise/ trust	Previous neglect leading to being behind
Sin/ "old self"	Impatience, pride	Anger, temper explosion,	When I'm tired I throw a fit
"New attitude of mind"/ Truth	Consider others as more important than own (Phil 2:3)	-Worth in God, perseverance (Hebrews 12:1-13) -Taming tongue (James 3:1-12)	God is merciful and loves me regardless of how I perform
"New self" / righteous behavior	-Praise friend -Ask for a turn -Play with other object -Pray for self-control	-Pray for dad/sister -Say kind words to sister -Express sadness in journal	-Admit it's hard -Choose rest: prayer, deep breaths, alone time
Armor of God for situation	Righteous-ness	Word of God, peace, faith	Peace

My Child

_____

(name and current date)

My hopes:

Personality:

Health/special needs:

Playing favorites:

Learning type: Loving type:

Challenging skill: Strong skill:

Try it!

The Word this week:

Prayer this week:

Worship this week:

Promises:

Nurturing:

Playing Plan:

My Child Example
(and Try it! On following page)

My Child: Chelsea, 2/1/20xx

My hopes: Reduce tantrums after school

    Personality: shy, sensitive

    Health/special needs: speech delay so she won't understand everything

    Playing favorites: My Little Ponies, Barbies, cars

    Learning type: visual

    Loving type: affection

    Challenging skill: understanding directions, fine motor skills

    Strong skill: telling stories, choosing

Try it! Example
(Related to My Child from previous page)

The Word this week:
By providing alone time with her Bible, and learn a song for 2 Corinthians 12:9-10:
> "But he said to me, "My grace is sufficient for you, for my power is made perfect in weakness." Therefore I will boast all the more gladly about my weaknesses, so that Christ's power may rest on me. That is why, for Christ's sake, I delight in weaknesses, in insults, in hardships, in persecutions, in difficulties. For when I am weak, then I am strong."

Prayer this week:

Give her peace and rest to wind down. In the morning before school: pray together for casting anxiety on God and restful afternoon

Worship this week:

Review schoolwork as giving glory to God (encourage current activity), make downtime, have worship music on

Playing Plan:
1. Set up ponies in classroom and model a pony who feels overwhelmed and then gets in car after school and tell mom pony she's tired and school was hard today. Have mom pony comfort and encourage her. Let Chelsea try.

2. Find a storybook about character struggling in school and read it together.

3. Finger paint emotions: messy does not equal bad. I'll say, "Let's pick a color and paint 'happy' on this page." Then one for confused, silly, and tired. Let her choose which order she does it.

Long Term Plan

	1st	2nd	3rd
Issue (hurt or sin)			
Ways to play to impart truth			
Things to go easy on while this is a focus			
Ways to affirm during this time			

Long Term Continued

	4th	5th	6th
Issue (hurt or sin)			
Ways to play to impart truth			
Things to go easy on while this is focus			
Ways to affirm during this time			

Journaling Check up

What issue have I worked on with my child this week?

What tools have I utilized (from Try it!)

How has it gone?

Are there times of day that work best?

What about times to avoid?

How did my child respond?

What can I adapt in my play-leadership to help facilitate better growth?

What can I adapt in my parenting to help facilitate better growth?

Through observation during playing, what progress has been made (either character, action, understanding, attitude) that I can praise in my child?

Through observation during playing, have any new signs of hurt of sin come up?

How can I learn more about this or address it?

Please take a moment to review this workbook on marketplaces online, in order to help parents decide if this is would help them.

Coming in 2015!

"Faith to Foster" is the working title for Jenn's next book, co-authored with her husband. This book is a narrative of how the couple engaged in foster care, how it called on their faith, and how American foster care works. Sign up for e-mail updates at www.jennmenn.com and follow Jenn on Twitter @Faithtofoster.

Bibliography

Adams, Jay E. 1970. Competent to counsel. Phillipsburg: P and R Publishing.

Chapman, Gary. Campbell, Ross. 2005. The Five Love Languages. Chicago: Northfield Publishing.

Demoss, Nancy. Gresh, Dana. 2008. Lies Young Women Believe. Chicago: Moody Publishers.

DivorceCare for Kids. Church Initiative.

Fitzpatrick, Elyse. Thompson, Jessica. 2011. Give Them Grace. Crossway.

Gottman, John. 1997. Raising an emotionally intelligent child. New York: Simon & Schuster Paperbacks.

Green, Steve. 2008. Hide 'Em in your Hearts CDs. EMI Label Group.

Jernberg and Booth. 2001. Theraplay, second Ed. San Fransisco: Jossey-Bass.

Rapada, Amy. 2007. The Special Needs Ministry Handbook: A church's guide to reaching children with Disabilities and their families. Booksurge Publishing.

Priolo, Lou. 1997. Heart of Anger. New York: Calvary Press.

Priolo, Lou. 2000. Teach Them Diligently. Woodruff: Timeless Texts.

Keck, Gregory. Kepecky, Regina. 2009. Parenting the Hurt Child. Colorado Springs: NavPress

Sande, Ken. 2002. Peacemaking for Families. Carol Stream: Tyndale House Publishers.

Tolbert, La Verne. 2000. Teaching like Jesus. Grand Rapids: Zondervan Publishing House.

Tripp, David. 2002. Instruments in the Redeemer's Hands. New Jersey: P&R Publishing.

Made in the USA
Lexington, KY
26 March 2015